Piano Interpretation
of the Seventeenth,
Eighteenth and
Nineteenth Centuries

Piano Interpretation of the Seventeenth, Eighteenth and Nineteenth Centuries

A Study of Theory and Practice Using Original Documents

Elena Letňanová

McFarland & Company, Inc., Publishers
Jefferson, North Carolina, and London

The present work is a reprint of the library bound edition of
Piano Interpretation of the Seventeenth, Eighteenth and
Nineteenth Centuries: A Study of Theory and Practice Using
Original Documents, *first published in 1991 by McFarland.*

LIBRARY OF CONGRESS CATALOGUING-IN-PUBLICATION DATA

Letňanová, Elena, 1942–
   Piano interpretation of the seventeenth, eighteenth and
nineteenth centuries : a study of theory and practice using
original documents / by Elena Letňanová.
     p.   cm.
   Includes bibliographical references and index.

   ISBN 978-0-7864-6708-2
   softcover : acid free paper ∞

   1. Piano — Methods — History.   2. Keyboard instruments —
Methods — History.   3. Piano music — Interpretation
(Phasing, dynamics, etc.)   4. Keyboard instrument music —
Interpretation (Phasing, dynamics, etc.)   5. Performance
practice (Music)   I. Title.
MT220.L495   2012
786.2'143'09 — dc20   91-52596

BRITISH LIBRARY CATALOGUING DATA ARE AVAILABLE

© 1991 Elena Letňanová. All rights reserved

*No part of this book may be reproduced or transmitted in any form
or by any means, electronic or mechanical, including photocopying
or recording, or by any information storage and retrieval system,
without permission in writing from the publisher.*

Front cover images: J.S. Bach (left), Frédéric Chopin, Franz Liszt;
cover design by David K. Landis (Shake It Loose Graphics)

Manufactured in the United States of America

McFarland & Company, Inc., Publishers
  Box 611, Jefferson, North Carolina 28640
  www.mcfarlandpub.com

*This book is dedicated to
Doctor Tibor Szász, concert pianist*

Contents

Introduction ix

1. Predecessors of the Piano   1

2. French Methods of the Seventeenth
   and Eighteenth Centuries   5

   François Couperin: *L'Art de toucher le clavecin*   7

3. German Treatises of the Eighteenth Century   37

   Carl Phillip Emmanuel Bach: *Versuch über die wahre Art das Klavier zu spielen*   38
   Daniel Gottlob Türk: *Klavierschule oder Anweisung zum Klavierspielen für Lehrer und Lehrnende*   66

4. Johann Sebastian Bach and
   Wolfgang Amadeus Mozart   87

5. Frédéric Chopin and Franz Liszt   101

6. German and French Treatises of the
   Nineteenth Century   141

   Adolph Kullak: *Die Aesthetik des Klavierspiels*   141
   Mathis Lussy: *Traité de l'expression musicale*   153

Appendix: The Development of the Elements   171

Notes   173
Bibliography   179
Index   181

Introduction

My investigation undertakes to analyze keyboard methods employed in the seventeenth, eighteenth, and nineteenth centuries. It attempts to identify the process by which individual components of these methods made their appearance, the relationships between them, and the sources of as well as the driving forces behind each development.

Discussion will focus on systems elaborated by the most prominent authors of each period. I will be looking at each method as a whole as associated with a specific composer. Then within this context I will attempt to identify those elements of the system which are new and those which have been adopted or derived from previous authors. This approach will enable the reader to develop a more integrated view of the individual systems employed over the period under consideration.

The discussion not only looks back to the earliest appearance of individual elements of a method, but also points out those which have retained a positive methodological significance up to the present day. I will distinguish between methodological elements which are of a more general nature—elements, that is, which would also find application in the interpretation of contemporary music—and those which are of specific importance to interpretation of the keyboard music of a given century, or with reference to the particular composer who is the author of the instructions under consideration.

This study does not devote equal attention to each of the various methodological schools or works on methods. Some of the less important among them passed into oblivion even in their own time. If they represent no important advances, they will be only mentioned and briefly commented upon. I will be giving closer attention to those authors who bring us to important crossroads in the evolution of keyboard methods; in these instances, I will also include information concerning those sections of their works which deal with methods that are not altogether original. Again, this will help the reader to develop a clearer picture of the methodological and pedagogical practice of the time.

Original works of the authors under consideration here have provided the most important sources of information for this study. In the seventeenth and eighteenth centuries, of course, this concept of "methods" did not yet exist in the sense in which the term is understood today. Works on "methods" of this period concerned themselves as well with improvisation, counterpoint, and other areas of music theory and aesthetics. I will therefore be concentrating on those portions of these works which deal with keyboard methods as this term would be used and understood today.

In the case of a number of writers it becomes necessary to put a picture of their methods together from correspondence or secondary sources (reports and accounts of contemporaries). I have also consulted present-day analytical-historical works.

The works of the period under discussion here differ widely in organization and the sources are necessarily scattered and unsystematic. Were I to adhere too closely to the original presentations it would be difficult to trace the development of the individual elements of these methods. Accordingly, I will be describing the original organization of each work simply for the sake of factual accuracy, but then analyzing the work itself on the basis of present-day understanding and methodological categories. To retain some of the original flavor of these works, however, I have included a number of direct quotations.

For purposes of systematic evaluation of each method, I have adopted the following organization: First, a discussion of *keyboard technique,* divided into the following components: posture at the instrument; position of wrists, palms, and fingers; tone production; control of hand muscles and relaxation; the motor aspect of execution; and finger mechanics. These components will be discussed in the order most logically related to their coverage in the original.

This discussion will be followed by an analysis of the method's instructions for *interpretation,* broken down into the following elements (again, discussion proceeds in an order logical to the original): dynamics; tempo; agogics; rhythm; phrasing (musical punctuation); articulation (mode of sequencing different touches within the framework of the phrase); ornamentation; fingering; and use of pedals and register.

If the work of a particular author does not recognize an element included here, that element will of course be omitted from the discussion.

It is hoped that through this description of the development of the methods the reader can begin to comprehend the general patterns in the evolution of keyboard practice.

INTRODUCTION

The greatest value of this study consists in its potential for pedagogical application. First, the music of the eighteenth century is becoming increasingly popular. Proper understanding of this music also offers a key to the comprehension of later forms of musical expression. To develop a true understanding of the music of this century, mere knowledge of the musical notation is not enough; one must also know the various modes of interpretation. And these, in turn, can best be followed through study of the contemporary methods. The methods of classical interpretation should constitute an integral component of musical education.

As it moves into a discussion of the nineteenth century, this study takes on additional meaning. The concept of piano method as it is understood today originated in the nineteenth century under the general term "piano school," and itself expresses the separation of the pianistic art or method from the field of compositional theory and methods of other instruments. The nineteenth century was a period of extensive development in the art of the piano. The literature for the piano became progressively richer, the new compositions developed the technical abilities of the performers to the point of creating a new vocation, a new type of instrumentalist, the virtuoso. Thus an entirely new type of piano school originated in the nineteenth century.

The first chapter in this study describes old musical instruments. The touch, the way each instrument is played, and even the type of music written for it are going to vary from one instrument to another. To comprehend the methods of earlier centuries will therefore require a grasp of the basic tonal and mechanical characteristics of the contemporary keyboard instruments, which this chapter attempts to provide.

The second chapter is devoted to the French methods of the seventeenth and eighteenth centuries and to the work of François Couperin in particular.

The third chapter deals briefly with the German methods of the eighteenth century and concentrates on the works of C. P. E. Bach and Daniel Gottlob Türk.

The fourth chapter will be looking at the methodological, pedagogical and interpretational conceptions of the most important composers of the eighteenth century, Johann Sebastian Bach and Wolfgang Amadeus Mozart. The fifth chapter takes us into the nineteenth century with a discussion of the methods of Frédéric Chopin and Franz Liszt. These four composers authored no fully elaborated works on methods; I will therefore attempt to derive their thinking on keyboard methodology from secondary sources.

The sixth chapter will then focus on written methodical works of the nineteenth century. In their time these works were thought of as closed and complete systems, which would be able to persist through time. Neither of these systems is based upon hypotheses. My concern in this chapter is to critically select from these works of the aesthetics of piano performance. Adolph Kullak's (1823-1862) *Aesthetiks* represents a crystallization of the views on piano performance of the German School of the nineteenth century. Mathis Lussy's (1828-1910) theoretical treatise summarizes the development in knowledge of interpretation in France in the second half of the nineteenth century. Lussy's essay is not written only for pianists, but has broad application among all types of musicians. The statements of Kullak and Lussy have been analyzed, criticized, sometimes dissected, but they have survived the fire of their contemporary critics and remain for us to examine.

1. Predecessors of the Piano

The Clavichord

In terms of the general system of classifying musical instruments, we include the clavichord among the stringed, percussion and hammer instruments with keys. An instrument older than the harpsichord, it appears at the end of the fourteenth century[1] in the form of a rectangular case and was initially played with the case resting on a table; later, in its prime (1500–1700), the clavichord had its own supporting framework in the form of slender, shaped legs. The case contained copper strings under tension and the action. The fifteenth-century version had a keyboard of three octaves (from D to e^2); by the eighteenth century the range was five octaves.[2] The player depressed the key, to the end of which was mounted a small tongue of brass. This tongue, or tangent, would strike the string from below, causing it to vibrate. The tone thus produced had a weak, subdued sound, so that only with difficulty could it be heard at the opposite end of a room. Although the clavichord could produce only a tone of this quality, the tone could be varied in intensity (it could be to some slight degree either diminished or augmented at the will of the player), and it was also possible to manipulate the sound produced by the string after it had been struck (vibrato), which is not possible with either the harpsichord or the piano. To modulate the tone in this way, the player would hold the finger on the depressed key and simultaneously pivot it around the tip, thereby producing a variation in pitch similar to the vibrato achieved on a stringed instrument.[3] This imparted a particularly appealing quality to the tone and extended its duration. This type of touch was referred to in Germany as *Bebung* (vibrato).

The advantages this instrument offered—pleasing melody lines and largely undifferentiated dynamics—destined it for the intimate occasion. It became an extremely popular instrument in Germany. The drawbacks, on the other hand, demonstrated that over the long run it was not going to be able to compete with the hammerclavier. Compared with the harpsichord, its tone was too weak. Because of its unassertive sound it was unsuitable for the salon. On the other hand, it proved to be particularly well suited for instruction. The best teachers and musicians of the eighteenth century valued it as the only keyboard instrument on which the student could develop a singing tone and, most importantly, learn to play with deep expression.

For formal concerts in the salons and palaces, the harpsichord was found to be more suitable.

The Harpsichord

The harpsichord may be traced back to origins almost simultaneous with those of the clavichord, with the harpsichord appearing just somewhat later in the fourteenth century. In external form it reminds us of the piano, but it had an entirely different action and produced tones of an entirely different timbre. Tones were produced not by a tangent striking the strings, as we have seen in the case of the clavichord, but rather by a sharp crow's quill which plucks them. The tone thus produced was stronger and more bell-like than that of the clavichord but was of shorter duration. It was not affected by the sharpness of the attack. The harpsichord produced a tone of uniform intensity, regardless of how hard or how gently the player depressed the keys. It required a rapid, energetic attack; if the player struck the keys too gently or indecisively, he obtained no effect whatsoever. The instrument would remain silent. The introduction of two keyboards and registration in the form of pedals offered the possibility of stepping the sound produced up or down in intensity as well as of altering the timbre. By manipulating the pedal registers the player could vary the color of the instrument. Other registers sounded the octave, even though the player would depress only a single key. "The cembalo originally had a range of almost three octaves, H–a^2."[4] This range was later (around 1700) extended to five octaves, F–f^3.[5]

Despite the fact that the harpsichord produced a tone which permitted no dynamic variation, this tone did possess a certain appeal, which lay in the sharpness and clarity of each individual note. Rhythmic precision and subtly differentiated articulation gave the instrument added power of expression. It permitted the employment of agogic effects as well; witness Couperin's thinking concerning the performance of his preludes in his *L'Art de toucher le clavecin*.

Comparison of the Two Instruments

The differences in the construction of the clavichord and the harpsichord played a role in determining the possibilities each offered with respect to both interpretation and technique (differences in touch, different dynamic potential). All this must be taken into consideration in playing the keyboard compositions of the seventeenth and eighteenth centuries, particularly if the player wants to preserve the authentic sound of the clavichord or harpsichord in his playing. With its more sensitive keyboard, the clavichord was capable of expressing the most subtle of emotions. "The harpsichord with its impersonal, rustling, quality offered greater scope for virtuoso performance."[6] The clarity and sharpness of its sound made it particularly suitable for pearly, effervescent passages, trills and a variety of ornaments, as well as for frequent changes in articulation at rapid tempo. Stepped variations in dynamics could be achieved over the longer lines, while with the registers the harpsichordist disposed of a range of timbres. Old methods suggested that instruction be given on both instruments, the clavichord being particularly suited for the development of interpretational skills, the harpsichord enabling the student to strengthen the attack of the individual fingers.

Instrumentation ad Libidum

It is not the intent here to go into any detail on the question of which works were written for which of the old instruments—which for the harpsichord, for example, and which for the clavichord. There were no separate bodies of literature for the different instruments at that time. What one needs to point out here is simply that, if the composer himself has not indicated the instrument for which a piece has been written, the interpreter can make this decision for himself.

It has been argued that it is entirely pointless today to try to take account of the potentials offered by the various old instruments and then to attempt to duplicate the sound of these old instruments on the keyboard instruments of today (Neuganz). This may be a legitimate argument, but it is a view which a great many pianists do not share, and the notion that the characteristic features of the clavichord and harpsichord should indeed be taken into account is an entirely legitimate one as well. There would be no point, of course, in concerning ourselves with works which have clearly and unambiguously been composed for the harpsichord (the works of Couperin and Rameau, for example). When we come to Bach's work, on the other hand, the situation becomes more complicated. One would have to have doubts in this instance, because it is only a small number of his compositions which he himself specifically indicated had been written for the harpsichord. I myself am of the view that the choice of instrument is not important; one can choose whichever instrument one wishes: clavichord, harpsichord or, for that matter, the modern piano as well. In some instances (as would be the case with the Goldberg Variations for harpsichord, for example), it is the technical difficulties — the crossing of voices and complex ornamentation — which almost call for the harpsichord. Other works, such as the Minuet Trio from the Little Preludes, the three-part inventions in E minor and C minor, the Prelude and Fugue in E minor from the first part of the *Well-Tempered Clavier*, and compositions similar in nature sound good on the clavichord. As played on the harpsichord without crescendi and diminuendi, these compositions lose their distinctive characteristics.

Harpsichord and Clavichord Technique

The methods of the time establish no distinction between harpsichord technique and clavichord technique. They are based on the same principles. The manuals on the subject contain no instructions which would make it clear that the harpsichord must be played differently from the clavichord. For neither instrument does the attack require movement of the entire hand; the player moves only the fingers. There were two reasons for this:

1) A light touch was sufficient to produce a tone on the clavichord. Tones were produced on the harpsichord by a rapid and energetic attack.

2) As compared with the keyboard of today's piano, the keyboard of both instruments had shallow depth by attack and lighter resistance when playing.

To perform the musical literature written for the clavichord and harpsichord the finger technique was therefore entirely adequate. As shall be seen later, this finger technique remained unchanged until the end of the eighteenth century.

There are works in the methods literature of the eighteenth century which treat a broader range of questions, such as those which analyze hand mechanics *(Motorik)* — that is, that element of technique concerned with the mechanics of the hand as a unit. These works have lost none of their penetration and today are not only of historical interest but highly instructive as well.

2. French Methods of the Seventeenth and Eighteenth Centuries

Conditions in seventeenth- and eighteenth-century France were particularly favorable for the development of harpsichord playing. One can look to a number of factors to account for this.

1) Lute playing had played an important role in the evolution of the French musical tradition. The literature for this instrument, as well as performance on the lute itself, had reached high levels of refinement as early as the sixteenth and seventeenth centuries. The harpsichordist of the eighteenth century could therefore pick up and continue this development in terms of both musical forms and manners of interpretation.

An example of the "lute structure":
The Sarabande by J. Ch. Chambonnières (1602–1672).

2) Just as important had been the tradition in organ music. The literature composed for organ and harpsichord was intimately linked to the performing art not only in France but also in Italy, Spain, and Germany. Music composed for the harpsichord was therefore for a long period of time associated with the literature for the organ[1]; then over the course of the seventeenth century it began to evolve its own characteristics. More closely related were compositions for the lute. Unlike the organ style, the harpsichord style is not tied to a rigorous polyphony. The phrase is full of movement, the more extended tones of the melody being elaborated with short embellishments and figures. Because tones produced on the harpsichord could not be sustained, composers were forced to circumvent this shortcoming by reproducing the sound and breaking up the chord structure. And this the performer found in the literature for the lute as well.

3) The age of Louis XIII and Louis XIV saw the French noble and royal courts, unlike the German, inclined toward an artistic taste whose characteristics were distinguished by subtlety, lightness, clarity, and refinement. And the harpsichord was precisely the instrument which best corresponded to the prevailing taste.

4) Interest in playing the harpsichord had begun to grow rapidly as early as the beginning of the seventeenth century. This required the development of an appropriate instructional literature. As a more highly developed instrument, the harpsichord ultimately began to displace the lute and over the course of the eighteenth century took over this place of preference entirely.

The extensive literature available for this instrument and the popularity of harpsichord playing led to the emergence of a school, a group of authors and interpreters, in France as early as the first half of the seventeenth century. This period saw a number of authors turn their attention to the development of manuals on methods. The first book of instruction appeared in 1650, a manual for harpsichord by Jean Denis entitled *Traité de l'accord d'épinette avec la comparaison de son à la musique vocal.* The year 1702 saw the appearance of a more important work, *Les principes du clavecin* by Michel St. Lambert (1613-1696), a court composer and lutenist.

The studies referred to here contained general discussions of the harpsichord and specific instructions for the harpsichordist. The problems these works resolved, however, remained few: fingering and the execution of the embellishments, which at the time were adequate to the demands of the compositions of the authors who wrote these methods. The works did not satisfy requirements for broader application and so for this reason will be of no further concern here.

In 1724 Jean Philippe Rameau published his *Méthodes pour la mécanique des doigts ou l'on enseigne les moyens de se procurer une parfaite execution sur cet instrument* (Methods of Finger Mechanics Which Offer Instruction in the Means of Developing Perfect Execution on This Instrument). A revised edition of this work appeared in 1732 under the title *Dissertation sur les differentes méthodes d'accompagnement pour le clavecin ou l'orgue* (Essay on Different Methods of Accompaniment for the Harpsichord or Organ). Both works deal primarily with technical problems of execution, which would follow from the rubric: Mechanics of the Basic Finger Movements. Despite the fact that quality and mode of attack, which he does discuss, would be included among the elementary components of musical expression, Rameau gives no attention to questions of interpretation. His work elaborates his own method of instruction for beginning harpsichordists and discusses the art of accompaniment and improvisation. Instruction proceeds from the outset on the basis of the five-finger position at the keyboard. Most of the methods employed over the course of the nineteenth and twentieth centuries have adhered to this mode of instruction. In developing musicality, Rameau stresses first and foremost the importance of an active improvisation and a feel for harmony. In view of the fact that Rameau gives no consideration to the individual elements of interpretation, Rameau's work will not be gone into in any greater detail.

The most important product of the French harpsichord art of the first half of the eighteenth century is a work by François Couperin (1668–1733), the court composer, organist, harpsichordist and teacher of Louis XIV. That work was entitled *L'Art de toucher le clavecin.*

François Couperin: *L'Art de toucher le clavecin*

One of the first treatises devoted to harpsichord keyboard practice was Couperin's *L'Art de toucher le clavecin.* Michel de Saint-Lambert's *Les principes du clavecin* (1702) should actually be considered the earliest work on harpsichord method, but Couperin's work occupies a particularly important place for two basic reasons:

1) It is, in a certain sense, the first complete method to deal with all the most essential problems of interpretation on the harpsichord in the first half of the eighteenth century; and

2) it is important because of who wrote it.

Couperin first published this by no means voluminous treatise in Paris in 1716. What was the critical factor in his decision to publish? He was played and recognized abroad, particularly after the appearance of his first book of compositions for the harpsichord *(Premier livre de pièces . . .).*

Intense interest was developing throughout Europe in his ideas on music, particularly in his conceptions concerning the interpretation of his own work. It was true that others of his time were already writing on methods (Ch. de Chambonnières, G. G. Nivers, 1665; J. H. D'Anglebert, 1689; M. de Saint-Lambert, 1702; J. Fr. Dandrieu, 1724; J. P. Rameau, 1724), but there were still no established, binding rules governing the performance of French compositions for the harpsichord. This called for some additional commentary from Couperin. Thus appeared his own method. When Couperin wrote this work, of course, he had no idea that it would ultimately establish itself as an important method and become the criterion for an entire era of harpsichord keyboard art. He wanted his observations to be seen only as offering a particular interpretation of his works, in the form here of short lessons. These were the product of his long years of study and continuous application in practice.

For purposes of the present study reference will be made to the French text of *L'Art de toucher le clavecin* published in 1933 by VEB Breitkopf & Härtel Musikverlag, Leipzig. This edition is based entirely upon the original printing of Couperin's text, which is now preserved in the Prussian State Library in Berlin.

In accordance with the practice of the time, this 47-page work began with a dedication to the king, recommendations from prominent contemporary musical figures in favor of publication, and then an introduction to the work itself. In terms of organization, the study is short on structure; measured against today's standards, what structure there is would strike one as unusual and bordering in places on the unsystematic. The sentences are sometimes extremely complex and sometimes very simple. Problems are not always formulated clearly. Considerations of the technical arcana associated with the art of interpretation are tied in with discussions of a more general nature.

To provide the reader an overview of the method under consideration here, the contents of Couperin's work will now be outlined:

    Foreword

    The present method outlined

    A brief discussion of fingering to enable the student to master the embellishments contained herein

    Embellishments employed in practice

    Grounds for preferring the new type of appoggiatura [*port de voix*]

Short preliminary exercises to develop the hands which will contribute importantly to good playing

Allemande

A discussion of this contradiction

Brief remarks on correct fingering which apply to many situations included in my two books [*Livres de pièces*...]

First prelude

Remarks and observations

Explanations of embellishments and signs

For purposes of the present study such headings will be used as are employed in the original version; others had to be deduced from the text. The original text does not always divide the individual sections with headings, but a certain logical relationship between sections which would stand complete in themselves becomes apparent.

What is the distinguishing characteristic of this work? Couperin himself stresses in the introduction that the basic theme of his presentation is beautiful playing on the harpsichord. "The method I am offering here is the only one of its kind and bears no relationship whatsoever to tablature, which is nothing more than a science of numbers; what I am dealing with first and foremost here is the art of fine playing on the harpsichord [as based upon demonstrated principles]."[2] Couperin explicates the style appropriate to the harpsichord. The work is written not only for the beginner, but for specialists and interpreters with artistic background as well. The following is a brief outline of the Couperin method:

ornaments as enhancements of performance

short preliminary exercises to develop the hands, which will contribute importantly to good playing

observations on good fingering, which pertain to many points in my two books [*Livres de pièces*]

eight preludes progressively organized with a view to achieving the desired advancement

observations on the development of stylistic orientation and

miscellaneous reflections.

Following the introduction and short outline are observations of a theoretical and practical nature, which one can break down systematically as follows: general questions of performance technique, methods employed at the beginning of instruction, plan of instruction, and exercises.

Let us now look at the first point and the technical aspect of keyboard performance. For his time, Couperin concerned himself with general questions in an unusually detailed, comprehensive manner—instrument selection, the age of the interpreter, tablature (notation), proper posture at the instrument and the position of the hands. On the age of the interpreter: "The best age at which to allow children to begin instruction would be the sixth or seventh year. This should not be understood to exclude older individuals; but to mold and shape the hands for playing the harpsichord, the earliest possible beginning, of course, would be the best...."[3]

Concerning instrument selection: "The very young should begin their instruction on either the spinet or one manual of the harpsichord and on these two instruments only, with both fitted with very light quills."[4] Light quilling would correspond to the term "light keyboard" which we use today with reference to the piano. Couperin's observation is of some importance: since children have weaker hands and fingers than adults, they are forced to execute a forceful attack at the harpsichord prematurely. As a consequence, they tire quickly, the fingers grow stiff and, occasionally, the entire locomotor apparatus may be affected.

On tablature (notation):

> Children should be presented with the tablature only after they actually have a certain number of pieces in their fingers. For the fact is that while children look at the book, it is almost impossible not to let their fingers get out of proper position and not to make contortions with them. Even if the ornamentation does not suffer from this, the memory will ordinarily develop better if the student learns material by heart.[5]

After children have mastered the minimum, that is, the preliminary exercises, they familiarize themselves with the notation—tone designations on the keys, intervals and so on—so that they will be able to play from memory and not from the tablature, which Couperin says contributes to better development of the memory.

As far as proper body position at the instrument is concerned, we know that this is one of the most critical preconditions for instruction. It must be a posture which permits unrestricted movement of both the muscles and the body as a whole. Prescriptions for proper body posture have varied with the individual stylistic periods. In Couperin's view:

> An adult should seat himself approximately 9 inches [roughly one-fourth of a meter] from the keyboard. This distance would be decreased correspondingly for younger people. The center of the body should be aligned with the center of the instrument.[6]

This prescription would apply to modern-day practice as well. One frequently sees players, particularly children, seated at the keyboard without proper alignment between the midpoint of the body and the midpoint of the instrument.

> The player should seat himself at the harpsichord such that the body is slightly turned to the right. The knees should not be pressed too closely together. The feet should be kept side by side, but with the right foot especially, well out.[7]

Today these requirements seem incomprehensible. They would make sense only in the case of music written in the two highest octaves on the keyboard (C^3–C^5) and presuppose notation restricted to this range. We must look for the connections, rather, in the courtly conventions of the time and not in the keyboard range of the harpsichord then in use (C–f^3).

Concerning hand position as a factor in good performance technique Couperin writes the following:

> The player should be seated at a height such that the undersurface of the elbow, the wrist and the fingers form a straight line. He should therefore use a chair which permits fulfillment of this requirement. Young people should have a pillow of a thickness which corresponds to the state of their physical development placed under their feet such that the feet do not dangle in the air and so as to allow the player to keep the body properly balanced.[8]

Couperin's thinking concerning hand position remains alive today in the interpretation of works both of his own time and of the classical period. It is interesting to note that Couperin's commentary here is not only a description of common practical experience, but an observation of certain logical relationships as well.

In the history of the development of method, tone formation (touch) was of truly revolutionary importance. Writers on methods had heretofore shown no interest in the beauty of the tone. In Couperin's view, three factors contributed to the beauty of a tone: the delicacy of the touch, the distance from which the player attacked the keys, and the suppleness and mobility of the fingers.

> The beauty with which one plays [*la belle execution*] will be much more a function of the suppleness and mobility [*liberté*] of the fingers than of the force applied. If a child is allowed to play on two manuals from the very beginning, it will unavoidably strain his small hands to produce sound from the strings; this will result in bad hand position and harshness in execution. A delicate touch depends also on holding the fingers as close to the keys as possible. Experience aside, it is reasonable to assume that a hand which attacks the keys from a height is going to produce a sharper tone than one which approaches them from a point closer to the keyboard and that [in the first instance] the quill will produce a harder tone from the string.[9]

In a later chapter of this study it will be seen that, entirely apart from the application of this principle in present-day methods, particularly for those passages in which a pearly, singing tone is desired, the touch suggested by both J. S. and C. P. E. Bach is based upon the same principles as those advanced by Couperin.

What follows are Couperin's instruction on hand mechanics *(Motorik)* and maximum mobility of the hand. In Couperin's day, the physiological-anatomical aspect of keyboard execution had not yet been studied. It was only in the twentieth century that students of method placed this question on the agenda (Steinhausen, Breithaupt). Couperin's observations concerning cramped nerves (that is, the cramping of the muscles) were of enormous value for the development of contemporary keyboard practice. Rameau enlarged upon Couperin's requirement for free movement of the muscles of the entire hand and body.

> Since they can have developed bad habits or hardened sinews, students who begin late, or who have been poorly instructed, must take care to loosen their fingers before they sit down at the harpsichord; that is, they must stretch the fingers, or have someone stretch them, in all directions [*c'est active se tirer, ou se faire tirer les doigts de tous les sens*]. This also stirs up the spirit and makes the student feel freer.[10]

These requirements could be taken from any present-day method. Couperin gives practical instructions for physical finger exercises and relaxing cramped finger muscles. Right down to the last few minutes before a performance, pianists will pay particularly close attention to relaxation precisely in order to keep their fingers limber.

Following the introductory commentary comes the real core of Couperin's treatise, that is, the subjects of fingering and ornamentation. But before turning for a detailed look at these central problems concerning methods, the methodological approach Couperin employed in his own practice will be reexamined. Following general principles of elementary theory and practice, he proceeds to the playing of the first exercises, "Little Exercises for Formation of the Hands." These initial exercises concentrate on the following drills:

1) ornamentation (trills, mordents, appoggiaturas, etc.)
2) single-voice progressions (sequences of three tones)
3) progressions of three to eight tones
4) sequences of trills and mordents
5) tremolos of varying intervals
6) broken chords ("batteries")
7) runs of thirds
8) a new way to play thirds in sequence (with slur).

Departing from the older style of playing without the slur, Couperin begins with the simplest keys and advances through the more difficult ones (that is, the keys with increasing numbers of sharps and flats), to virtuoso pieces. There is really no need to go into the advisability of this particular approach. Included below for purposes of illustration are excerpts from the "Little Exercises for Forming the Hands" containing ascending and descending progressions. These drills are based upon three tones as compared with Rameau's five-tone progressions of fifths. All progressions illustrated here are gradually introduced in all keys over the course of instruction.

Progressions of thirds ascending and descending (the soprano key is to be read a big third lower from the middle C):

Progressions of fourths ascending and descending:

Progressions of sevenths:

The octave scales (referred to today simply as "scales") retain the old fingering with substitution, whereby the longer fingers are laid over the shorter ones, that is, 3 4, 3 4 ascending and 3 2, 3 2 descending. This fingering reminds one of that employed in playing the lute.

Scales with Couperin's new fingering (the thumb and the fingers crossed over the thumbs were not yet in use at this time; the use of three or four fingers sufficed—/2, 3, 4/, /2, 3, 4, 5/:

Progressions of mordents with slur (legato)[11] ascending and descending. (Transpose the notation a third lower.) The right hand:

By means of a finger substitution on the same key in the example shown here Couperin shows that he preferred a legato style of playing and was attempting from the very beginning of his course of instruction to help the student develop a *cantabile* style of rendering the melody line.

The left hand:

Example A below shows the execution of progressions of thirds in the old style of playing without slur with the stereotypical fingering $\frac{4}{2}$, $\frac{4}{2}$ *etc.*

Example B shows for the first time Couperin's new way of binding the thirds together (legato).[12]

The last example shows that Couperin did not obstinately insist on adherence to the old maxims.

Following exercises with embellishments and the three- to eight-tone sequences, the student moved on to drills involving the execution of scales and thirds in all keys. The last technical pattern to which Couperin introduced his students was the chord and its broken forms, what were referred to as batteries (arpeggios). The origins of the batteries may be found in the Italian sonatas *(sonades)*.

b.

After the student has mastered the purely mechanical aspects of execution, the individual tones and the forms which follow, he moves on to a course of instruction in theory. Provided that in the introductory phase of the instruction in theory he has developed a solid grasp of the intervals in all keys, the perfect and imperfect cadences, the chords and the figuring for the bass, the student now begins gradually to make his way through the intricacies of key theory. In Couperin's view, the knowledge of harmony constitutes "a kind of local memory," by which he surely means the musical memory, which gives the young harpsichordist more confidence and helps him consciously to get himself back on track when he makes a miscue. This is the first reference anywhere to the musical memory in a treatise on methods.

Methodological procedure has now been laid out. What is important now is the question of "how" the student should practice. Couperin's answer is similar to what one would hear from a present-day instructor: "Before the student proceeds on to the short exercises . . . care must be taken to insure that the trills, mordents, appoggiaturas, arpeggio-sequences and runs are practiced very slowly. . . ."[13] As can be seen from the short method plan, these exercises constitute the basis from which the student can advance to a study of the first independent compositions, the preludes. "[A]nd the pieces themselves cannot be learned too carefully,"[14] by which Couperin is referring to the emphasis to be placed on slow and careful execution.

Couperin's plan of instruction emerges from a modest comment between the lines of the method:

> Once the student can play six pieces varying in nature in accordance with all the rules, he will be able to play many others of the same type: particularly in the case of a younger student, a larger number will invariably inject a certain element of untidiness as a consequence, of which he can rid himself only at the cost of a great deal of effort.[15]

Couperin stresses the most important aspect of the student's performance, that is, the cleanness of his execution, which strikes today's performer as simply emphasizing the obvious. This is indeed a critical problem. One has only to observe how many students are capable of learning and of playing "cleanly" and what a problem this is even for the concert pianist.

The two most important problems, fingering and ornamentation, which constitute the core of Couperin's treatise, will now be examined.

FINGERING

When one considers the *Short Essay on Fingering*... one must bear in mind the fact that Couperin was one of the first to introduce a modern fingering system. By the term "modern" here is meant a system which attaches as much importance to the thumb as to the other fingers of the hand and which introduces a new numbering for the fingers.[16] The old system of so-called German Colorists Conrad Paumann, Hans Buchner, Elias Nicolaus Ammerbach and others used 0 for the thumb, 1 for the second finger, 2 for the third finger, 3 for the fourth finger, and 4 for the little finger.

Couperin was the first to assess accurately the intimate relationship between fingering and tone quality. This is illustrated by the following example:

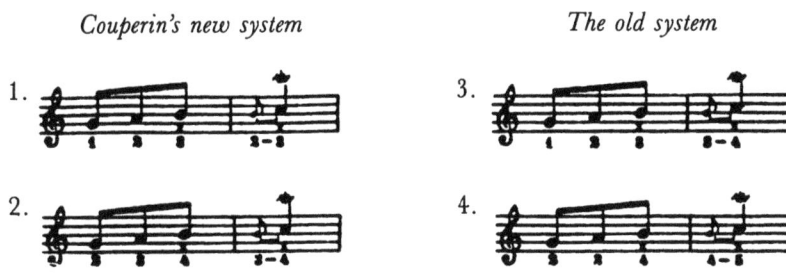

The first two examples, 1 and 2, illustrate Couperin's sensitive system of fingering as applied to ornamentation. The finger numbered 3 in example 3 and the finger numbered 4 in example 4 are forced to shorten, or to release early on, the last eighth note of the first measure to be able to articulate the grace note of the ornament in the second measure. Couperin's comments in this connection go to the very heart of this problem in interpretation. He writes as follows:

> I have demonstrated that I can tell without looking at the hands of the player whether the two trills in question have been played with one and the same finger or with two different fingers. My students have noticed the same thing. From this I conclude, basing myself on the majority of observations, that there is something to this.[17]

In all his observations on fingering, importance attaches to this one, which is consistent with the later remarks of both J. S. and C. P. E. Bach: Fingering here is based upon the natural characteristics of the hand and the varying strength and degrees of independence of the individual fingers. Many individuals exhibit "diminished ability to execute with certain fingers, when it comes to the execution of shakes"[18] for example. Couperin's advice that the player should nevertheless not neglect to develop the independence and flexibility of the individual fingers[19] through a well-rounded program of exercises is a modern view. He had in mind here the use of not only the more capable fingers, but of the weaker, less independent fingers as well.

Couperin's fingering also has a basis in phrasing. The fingering for "La milordine" in the *First Book for Harpsichord*, for example, is evidence in support of the thesis that fingering is based on phrasing and of the assertion that it is essential to make maximum use of all fingers. The first three measures of this example are fingered with a substitution (4–5) so as to make it possible to form Couperin's intentionally long phrase (in the right hand).

2. FRENCH METHODS

Another example demonstrates the precision of the linkage within a melody constituting a five-measure phrase.

Until Couperin developed his method, the progression of linked shakes had never been mentioned in any keyboard method.

In the "Reflections" which follow, Couperin introduces those passages from his book for harpsichord which he has provided with the appropriate fingering. These passages present the student with some truly thorny problems. Couperin lends a hand here with clarification of some ambiguous situations, thereby facilitating execution. From these specific instances one can draw conclusions for many other, similar cases. The composition entitled "Idées heureuses" from the *First Book for Harpsichord* offers an example of one of these challenging passages.

ORNAMENTATION

The second and most important problem the treatise addresses is the problem of ornamentation, to which Couperin devotes a brief chapter entitled "Ornamented Execution."

Before the specific types of ornamentation are looked at in greater detail, some problems associated with interpretation will be examined briefly.

The relationship between the printed notation and the actual execution of a work in Couperin's century differed substantially from what can be found to be the case in the succeeding century. Most important in this regard is the fact that the Baroque did not differentiate between composition and interpretation. Frescobaldi, Bach, Händel, Couperin, etc., were composers and interpreters in one person. Secondly, unlike present-day notation, the musical text as printed did not provide a precise and detailed elaboration of the composition, but rather established only a "framework" within which the improvisational art of the musician found its true expression. To execute the notation itself then means to complete the development of the melody in all its aspects, that is, to elaborate the ornamentation in conformity with specific rules, realize the figured bass and assume individual responsibility for the nature of the tempo, selection of the dynamics and the agogics, and everything having to do with phrasing and articulation. To the contemporary interpreter, these aspects of interpretation were so clear and easily grasped that the composer could leave them wholly or partly to the performer's taste and discretion.

Different ornament signs make their appearance at different times in different countries. The sign ⸯ over a note, for example, indicates not only a shake, but an appoggiatura, a small cluster, as well. But then the sign for a shake in England was ♩ or ⸯ, in Purcell's notation ⸯ, in France in Chambonier's system ⸯ, and in Germany ⸯ or ⸯ, not to mention all the other types of ornament. And then if one looks only at the sign for the same type of shake, it will be found to vary from one composer to another. The shake from above, that is, a shake with an upper supporting note, was indicated by the following signs: ⸯ in J. S. Bach, ⸯ in D'Anglebert, ⸯ in Marpurg, ⸯ in Purcell and ⸯ in Mondonville (Mondonville's sign indicating a suspension in the system of ornamentation employed by Couperin and Rameau, ornamentation which is referred to today as an agogic device).

Couperin attached great importance to the beauty with which a performer rendered the music. Ornamentation is one of the components of the performing art and factors in the aesthetics of keyboard performance. It was subject to the conventions and the trends in fashion, and, at least as far as his own work was concerned, Couperin wanted to define his ornaments precisely.

In his chapter entitled "Ornamentation," Couperin presents detailed descriptions, the various signs and the manner of execution of many different ornaments. It would be useful at this point to introduce the ornaments most frequently used not only in Couperin's works, but in the works of other composers as well. (It has been observed that students frequently fail to make the proper distinctions when it comes to this aspect of music.)

Concentration here will be on three types of mordents, two types of supporting notes (long appoggiaturas, to which Couperin refers as *ports de voix*), several types of shakes and the "ornaments" referred to as suspensions and aspirations.

The ornament employed most frequently by Couperin was the mordent. In the catalogue of ornaments it occupies first place.

a. The simple mordent *(pincé simple)* corresponds to what we refer to today as a mordent, indicated by the sign ⋏ .

This is a short mordent. The following are examples of long mordents.

b. Double mordent *(pincé double):*

c. Long mordent *(pincé continu):*

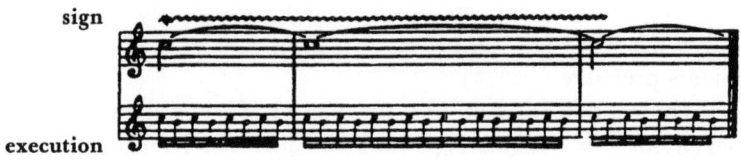

d. Mordent with accidentals:

In examples a, b and d it is clear from the composer's notation that the mordent is to be played before the main note. The following is an example from the chapter entitled "Agréments" (Ornamentation): "Each mordent should begin with the note over which it is written." Turning attention now to example b, one can observe that the mordent consists of auxiliary notes (small notes) and a final note (the main note). In this case, "both components of the mordent must share the value of the main note," as Couperin prescribes in his instructions. Among the mordents one should also include the mordent with supporting note (appoggiatura), but since Couperin grouped this ornament in the general category of "appoggiaturas" his example will be followed.

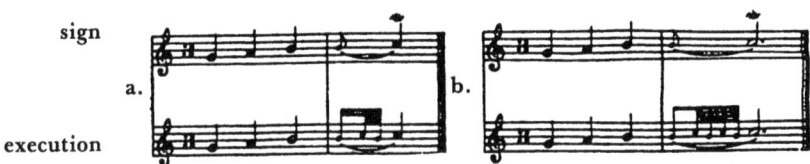

sign
a.   b.
execution

The logic behind Couperin's sign usage here is flawed. First of all, the appoggiatura is 1) neither simple (short) nor double (doubled, or long), but rather a mordent which is short (simple) and long (double); and 2) the ornament in the second measure of each one of these examples is not an appoggiatura, but a combination ornament: a mordent with appoggiatura, that is, a short mordent with appoggiatura (a) and a long mordent with appoggiatura (b). What Couperin refers to as a *port de voix coulée* (appoggiatura with slide), example c, can be considered a simple, that is, a true appoggiatura *(port de voix simple)* — that is, an appoggiatura from below.

c.

As far as examples a and b are concerned, even an authority such as Couperin can be charged with placing the small, indeterminate notes ahead of the main note: Reviewing here Couperin's basic rule of ornamentation, both the auxiliary notes and the main note of an ornament must share the value of the main note.[20] From examples a and b a relationship cannot be established between the appoggiatura from below and the mordent, nor in the case of example c can the relationship be established between the appoggiatura and the main note. The answer will appear only with C. P. E. Bach's celebrated *Essay,* which says that the auxiliary note takes from the main note a half of its rhythmic value if the when divided by three the auxiliary note takes ⅔ of main note value.

The other unknown factor involved in the execution of the combined ornaments, and of the appoggiaturas in particular, was the way these embellishments were to be incorporated into the surrounding musical structure, that is, with the bass. Couperin neglected no detail here. The auxiliary notes of the ornaments (particularly those of the appoggiatura), to include the combination ornaments, must be played simultaneously with the harmony and not before it.[21]

Another kind of ornamentation is the shake (tremblement). One is confronted with a variety of shakes in the interpretation of Couperin's works for the harpsichord. (This will be true of the works of other composers as well.) In the *Method* a number of them are marked "legato" *(tremblements liés);* others are not *(détaché)*. Still others of these ornaments will be of varying lengths—long *(tremblements continus)* and short. Then there are shakes with an auxiliary note above *(tremblement appuyé)* and others still which Couperin leaves undesignated, shakes so short they do not even include an auxiliary supporting note, not even a finishing note (here he was intending the inverted, or upper mordent, or *Pralltriller,* which still at that time was not indicated by its own sign).

Attention will be concentrated on the shakes which are commonly executed imprecisely, which makes for playing inappropriate to the desired style.

a. shake with legato   b. shake without legato

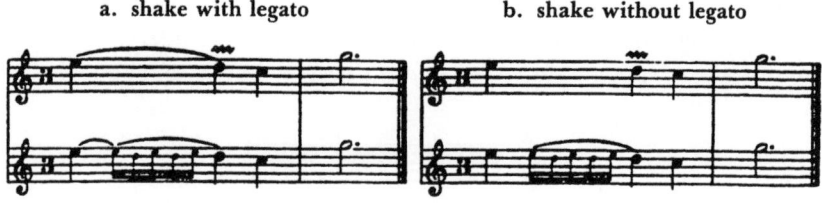

Both examples illlustrate Couperin's statement that "...if a shake is indicated over a note, it must always be begun with the main note [example a] or the half-tone above [example b]." In the case of example b, this would be the major second above, not the minor second, as he has written.

In the context of this discussion of the artistic aspects of keyboard performance, one more observation will be added here to round out this description of Couperin's nuanced playing and his practical instructional methodology. Although the shakes in Couperin's ornament table are shown as equal-valued devices, "they must nevertheless be begun more slowly than they end."[22] The increase in tempo must remain imperceptible.

This principle would apply above all to the third type of shake, the uninterrupted shake. And the final piece of advice concerning the way ornaments should be practiced is of no less importance than any of the foregoing: They should be practiced slowly and with all fingers. On this point Couperin is in agreement with the commentary of both C. P. E. and J. S. Bach.

Other ornaments may be found within the work of Couperin. In his own compositions, Couperin marked slides *(tierce coulé)* and executed them differently from his forerunners, contemporaries, and those who would follow.[23] The ornament was executed in a dotted rhythm. It is not known whether the ornament occurs before the main note. There is no indication of it in the *Method*. It is probably played simultaneously with the bass like the other ornaments (shakes, appoggiaturas). This conclusion may be drawn from Couperin's statement given on page 17 of his treatise.

The slide can be treated as the smallest of the slurs used in phrasing. Closer attention will be given to this device when Couperin's notation is dealt with in more detail, later in this chapter.

The term "accent" refers to the ornament now called the *Nachschlag*, springer, or acute, which is marked in the example by an "x."

Couperin marked his arpeggios so as to indicate whether the chord is to be broken upward or downward. In the dotted rhythm employed, the execution differs from present-day practice:

notation

execution

Couperin's *Method* includes no discussion of the short appoggiatura, or upper mordent *(Pralltriller)*, these devices being still in process of evolution during this period.

Attention will now be directed to suspension and aspiration, without which the interpretation of not only Couperin's works, but those of his contemporaries as well, would be inconceivable. This phenomenon was certainly to be found in earlier practice, but it was first identified by Couperin and classified as an ornament. From the vantage point of today, his commentaries on this ornament appear as the earliest references to the agogical devices, as the terminology would suggest. This phenomenon follows three directions simultaneously here and so cannot be incorporated neatly among the other artistic devices. What is interesting here is the fact that Couperin himself did not realize this and included it among the ornaments.

The assertion that the tone of the harpsichord is predetermined and incapable of any intensification or diminution was in Couperin's view untenable. His long years of practical activity, his studies, his formal education and his talent enabled him to discover a number of devices which could be employed to modify the tone of the harpsichord at least to some extent (subjectively), devices which, as Couperin himself put it, helped breathe a soul into this instrument. Couperin created this emotive mode of expression through the use of the two devices to be discussed in this section, devices which consist essentially in the introduction of irregularities into the pattern of articulation — namely, a shortening of the tone (what is referred to as an "aspiration") and an agogic delaying of the tone (the "suspension"). Employed at the appropriate times and places in a composition and properly adapted to the character of the piece, these two devices can be extremely effective. Couperin expresses himself on this point as follows:

> These two ornaments, by their contrast, leave the ear undetermined in such a way that, in those places where the bowed instruments would increase their tone, the suspension at the harpsichord, by a contrary effect, seems to produce this desired result.[24]

Accordingly, where the bow would intensify the tone, the harpsichord must retard the tempo slightly, thus prolonging the note (suspension), while at those points where the bow diminishes the tone, the harpsichord would introduce an aspiration. This device, therefore, has a dynamic effect, although only subjectively. Couperin offers the first guidelines to the execution of this dynamic-agogic device in the ornamentation chart included in his *Method*.

Suspension (delay of the note) is indicated by the ⩚ sign over the note and expressed by a pause. The pause before the note under the ornament sign will depend on the individual taste of the interpreter.

Describing the execution in nonmusical terms, one could say it would be akin to catching the breath before the note, which is slightly delayed.

notation

execution

In Couperin's view, the suspension will be employed only very rarely and then only in slow, tender compositions.

Jean Philippe Rameau, too, would use this type of ornament in the role of a pause, which would facilitate phrasing:

"Les Soupirs."—J. Ph. Rameau

Note here the use of the term *tendrement* ("tenderly").

In this particular example the suspension is combined with a second ornament.

Aspiration (interruption, or shortening, of the note) is shown in the next example:

notation

execution

The mark above notes a^1 and f^2 in the first line does not indicate the (shortest) staccato used today. It is, rather, an articulation sign indicating that the note is to be shortened by one-fourth of its value. As far as the aesthetic effect of the aspiration is concerned, the note under the ▼ sign "must be slightly detached in slow and tender passages and then executed more vigorously in the quick and light compositions."[25]

In these ornaments Couperin revealed the most essential devices used in his playing. Other facts were at work here as well. The art of playing the harpsichord was held in high esteem at this time. Harpsichord playing was also a widespread activity, and Couperin held the view that he should omit no detail which would contribute to artistic performance. He was very well aware of the fact that his ideas would be of benefit to those who were capable of appreciating them.

Most of the editions of Couperin's works for harpsichord from that century omit these effective ornaments. If it is not possible to play from the precious original editions, the effort should at least be made to obtain facsimile editions.[26]

INTERPRETING THE COMPOSITIONS — THE EIGHT PRELUDES

When the harpsichordist has surmounted the two most critical problems — fingering and the execution of the ornaments and technical patterns in all keys, in all possible forms and chords, to include the broken forms — and wishes to attain still higher levels of perfection, he should, to Couperin's way of thinking, spend two to three years on the purely technical studies. Only then should he proceed on to the study of accompaniment and the compositions, which he should play by turns. Why are students to begin their study of accompaniment only after two to three years? When it comes to the hand mechanics involved in playing the harpsichord, this prescription can be justified. "In playing accompaniment, after all, the right hand will always be occupied with playing the chords [chording], and this places the hand under a certain degree of tension. This causes stiffness and impairs the mobility the hand has acquired in previous work on the execution of the technical figures. The pieces learned first will therefore help avert this difficulty."[27]

The eight preludes from *L'art de toucher le clavecin* are the first compositions devoted to the study of interpretation which Couperin wrote in the keys of his works for harpsichord in Book I and Book II. The preludes are arranged in order of increasing difficulty and not only indicate the keys of the pieces to be played for practical purposes, but also help relax and loosen the fingers and try out instruments the student has not yet played.

Immediately striking in the first prelude (see page 27) are

1) the two voices in the right hand;
2) the striving for a legato, that is, a cantabile, style in execution, an effect achieved with the fingering (frequent substitution);
3) the limited ornamentation; and
4) the brevity of the prelude.

The second prelude (see page 28) is longer and, as compared with the eighth-note movement in the first prelude, the rhythmic struc-

First Prelude

ture is more differentiated (dotted rhythms). It contains a number of different ornaments and more of them (mordents, upper mordents, appoggiaturas). The simple imitations in the inner and outer voices and a number of scale passages constitute the touchstone here.

The first four preludes can be assigned to students of any age; only the very young, those who would not yet have developed the physical capacities for this, should not be expected to execute precisely the full range of notes comprising the fairly extended chords.

The preludes, from the artistic point of view, can be seen to constitute complete and perfect miniatures. They are polyphonic in structure and contain three- and four-voice figurations. They are lute-like in nature and, particularly in the case of the last preludes, exhibit a fairly differentiated rhythmic structure. Taken together, these factors make the preludes an effective introduction to the unique characteristics of the structure and texture of harpsichord music.

Attention will be turned here to the view of prelude form which prevailed in Couperin's time. He marks the first measure of the third prelude "mesuré" and "mesuré-lent," in opposition to non-measured free preludes, almost written like "aleatoric" notation with the essential melody and harmony structure. Couperin's thinking here makes it clear that measured time was invariably his practice. Even though a performer must adhere to the beat, the prelude is a composition free in its form and is to be played with an imagination. Couperin's conception of more exact measure is a reaction to the non-measured preludes of his predecessors and his contemporaries — Denise Gaultier, Louis Couperin, and Henry D'Anglebert.

28 2. FRENCH METHODS

Second Prelude

Prelude 1. in the notation of H. D'Anglebert and the interpretation of Thurston Dart:[28]

Prelude, notation in original by Louis Couperin:

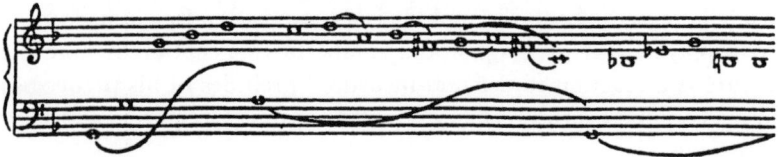

Third Prelude from François Couperin:

Couperin's "schematic" preludes can be seen as substitutes to be employed by those incapable of the more spontaneous realizations and improvisation. The most important reason why Couperin provided measures for the preludes was that he wanted to make them easier to read and learn. This detail offers an example related to method.

Musical examples found in his treatise include an extended, detailed discussion of the sound of the harpsichord and the violin, the advantages and drawbacks of these instruments and of compositions better suited to the harpsichord. He composed an allemande expressly for this purpose. The allemande represents the type of piece which is most suitable for the harpsichord, because there is continuous motion in both treble and bass.

Allemande

COMPARISON OF TWO MUSICAL CULTURES AND CRITICISM OF THE MUSICAL NOTATION

Couperin's observations on the subject of French and Italian musical notation are particularly valuable not only for the interpretation of Couperin's own works for the harpsichord in particular, but for the interpretation of the French musical literature in general. Couperin takes a critical view of the discrepancies to be found between French music as written and the realization of this notation in performance. He sees the roots of these discrepancies to lie in the fact that, unlike the Italian musical notation, the French notation corresponds to the style of the French language as written. On this point Couperin explains:

We [the French] employ a notation, of course, which is at variance with our actual execution; foreigners will for this reason play their own music better than they play ours. The Italians, on the other hand, write their music in the correct values, just as they have conceived it. For example, we will play a stepwise sequence of eighth notes as though they were dotted, but our notation will show them to be of equal value.[29]

In French music, notes of equal value were played as unequal (eighth notes or sixteenth notes written as of equal value, for example, were played as though they were dotted). If the composer wanted these eighth notes or sixteenth notes to be given equal value when played, he would have to give specific instructions to this effect or mark the text to indicate what today would be referred to as a staccato style. Accordingly, 𝄽𝄽𝄽𝄽 would indicate not four sixteenth notes to be played staccato, but rather four sixteenth notes to be given equal value.

A fragment from "La Badine" from the *First Book for Harpsichord* illustrates the discrepancy between interpretation and notation:

composer's notation

as played in Couperin's day

The eighth notes marked "x" in the composer's notation are interpreted differently (that is, as though dotted).

Couperin's table of ornaments contains another ornament, the *coulé*, which also illustrates the discrepancy between notation and execution. It can be found in "La Badine" on the first and second beats of the third measure and on the first, second and third beats of the fourth measure.

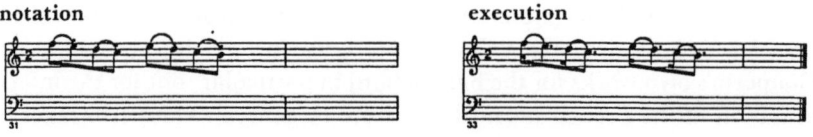

notation   execution

The slurs over the dotted notes indicate that each time the second and fourth notes of a melodic sequence of eighth notes are to be accentuated, the notation will be realized in a manner precisely the opposite of that employed today, where the slur indicates that the first note is to be accented, a dot indicating that the second note should be shortened, that is, played with a somewhat lighter attack. At the same time, as has been observed in the discussion on ornamentation, the ornament sign indicates a subtle articulatory device, a linkage of two tones, what is thought of today as the smallest unit of phrasing and referred to as a "drop and lift."

Couperin's efforts to eliminate the inconsistency between notation and execution would find support in the not-distant future from J. S. Bach. What he is striving for here is a system which will enable a composer to convey his musical ideas more completely. He writes in this connection as follows:

> Thus, not having devised signs or characters for communicating our specific ideas, we try to remedy this by indicating at the beginning of our pieces, by some such words as Tenderly, Quickly, etc. as far as possible the idea we want to convey. I hope that someone will take the trouble to translate us for the benefit of foreigners; and may it procure for them the possibility of judging of the excellence of our instrumental music.[30]

Today it is entirely obvious that tempo and expression should be indicated at the beginning of each piece together with pedaling and metronome settings, but in Couperin's day these markings were employed only rarely. Couperin's efforts helped to make musical notation more precise.

COUPERIN ON HARPSICHORD TEMPI

Couperin's observations on tempi are based in logic; that is, he proceeds on the basis of the sound of the instrument. Should one be inclined to disregard this ground, there are Couperin's long years of experience as both teacher and artist to confirm it. "Because of the limited duration of the tone of the instrument, the cantabile pieces should not be played on the harpsichord quite as slowly as they would be played on another instrument."[31] Rhythm and style can thereby remain independent of faster or slower tempi.

Once the student has mastered his practice preludes and the art of accompaniment, which he has now studied in turn, he can begin over the course of the next few years to study recital pieces, provided, of course, that he follows precisely all the rules Couperin has laid down. Taking as a basis what has been learned about Couperin up to this point, an attempt will be made to develop a judgment of what he held to constitute the essential

Table of Ornamentation

requirements for achieving the highest degree of perfection in artistic performance.

1. Through the vehicle of the allemande which he composed as a model for purposes of illustration, Couperin was attempting to set forth his view that the style which best suited the harpsichord should be maintained. This meant that the rapid passages and runs, the different forms of broken chords, the syncopated rhythms and the broken rhythms

employed in writing for the lute which were being transposed into works for the harpsichord were to be executed with the utmost precision. When it comes to the harpsichord style, one naturally prefers these passages and runs to the style of pieces which have been written in slower tempi with longer note values.

2. "In everything played on the harpsichord" one should strive to achieve a perfect legato to present the pieces with the proper tone. Passages for which a different articulation or fingering would not contribute to this effect would constitute exceptions here.

3. From the criticism of the musical notation employed by the composer and the chapter on ornamentation one can conclude that all ornaments are to be executed with maximum precision. "Combination ornaments with shakes should be played with a sense of proportion and at an imperceptibly increasing tempo."[32]

4. It follows from the chapter on the preludes that compositions with a set tempo must be played at a constant, regular tempo.

5. Concerning the agogic articulatory embellishments, the suspension and aspiration, it can be observed that Couperin does not permit extension of the duration of a note beyond its proper time value.

6. Stylistic form, finally, should "conform to contemporary standards of good taste, which is incomparably purer than the old."[33]

SUMMARY

Couperin's work on methods is of fundamental significance. Particularly in its exemplary breakdown of the general problems of harpsichord playing, it constitutes a basis for later keyboard methods. Couperin elaborates his theory on two levels: the theoretical and the practical. In all phases of instruction, as well as in artistic performance, both levels are inseparably linked. Couperin offers the first constructive guide to a true course in method, from the very beginning to the realm of polished artistic performance. In so doing he brought to completion the "progressive course in method" as outlined in the methods manuals of the sixteenth century (Spanish manuals by Juan Bermudo and Tomas de Santa Maria). Couperin thereby filled in the areas on the methodological map which had hitherto been explored either only very slightly or not at all.

In the area of keyboard technique this means:

1) development of an aesthetically pleasing tone; and
2) relaxation of hand movement at the keyboard.

This problem was given detailed attention in the anatomically and physiologically oriented works on methods of the early twentieth century. This source has inspired a whole series of methods and books.

As far as pleasing tone is concerned, Couperin knew what governed tone quality: the technique of the attack, of course, plus the relaxation of muscle movement. What he could not yet know, however, was that it is essential consciously to relax and control not only the movement of the fingers, but all movements and muscles of the entire locomotor apparatus. The harpsichord style required no power, all parts of the hand not yet having begun to participate in the motions involved in playing the instrument. Finger pressure alone sufficed for the most part. Couperin could not yet have known the technique of attacking the keys by striking them from above or using the entire hand. He therefore evaluated the utility or inutility of motions in relation to the fingers and, at most, the palm of the hand only.

Turning now to the perfection of finger technique from the point of view of the mechanics involved, Couperin's course in method was conceived and elaborated in every possible detail for the time. He begins with the simplest conceivable groupings, three tones, to which he gradually adds new ones, thus extending the reach of the hand. This enables the student to concentrate not only on the development of the strength of each of the fingers individually, but also, and most importantly, on the quality of his attack and the perfection of a legato style. If Couperin can be faulted, it would be only for the fact that his course of instruction does not include the intervals to be played with one hand (fourths, sixths, octaves, etc.), only thirds, and that the student practices these figures in one rhythmic pattern only.

Couperin's plan of instruction comprises six different compositions. For purposes of comparison, an example of a present-day practice program follows. This one is suggested by the methods specialist Ándor Földess in his *Keys to the Keyboard* (Oxford, 1950).

The Földess suggested weekly practice program

Monday	Tuesday	Wednesday	Thursday	Friday	Saturday
Beethoven sonata					
Part I	Part II	Part III	Part I	Part II	Part III
Chopin					
Étude A	Étude B	Étude C	A	B	C

Monday	Tuesday	Wednesday	Thursday	Friday	Saturday
Bach					
Prelude	Fugue	Prelude	Fugue	Prelude	Fugue
Contemporary work					
A	B	C	A	B	C
Technical exercises					
A	B	C	A	B	C
Sight reading	Repetition of repertoire continued in alternation				

This proposed practice program, of course, is only a model and so should not be taken literally. A longer Romantic composition could be substituted for a classical sonata, for example, or an étude by Liszt or Debussy for a Chopin étude. Both writers give equal emphasis to the importance of practicing in accordance with a specific program. A program devised by a good teacher can be interesting, and when followed with some degree of flexibility it can also increase the student's desire to study. The program must also, of course, be tailored to meet the individual requirements of the student.

Couperin's prescription for slow and precise practicing develops an ability to execute cleanly. The postwar works on methods come back frequently to the question of clean execution.

In the area of keyboard execution:

1) Couperin introduces the concept of respect for the notation; in this connection he criticized the contemporary treatment of the rhythm.

2) As far as ornamentation was concerned, he introduced signs with precise descriptions of the manner in which they were to be executed. He dealt only with certain ornaments, however. There is no mention, for example, of the upper mordent *(Pralltriller)* or of a number of other ornaments. Ornaments (compound appoggiaturas, shakes, arpeggios) were executed in a manner different from that employed today.

3) Couperin laid the foundations of agogics and introduced the elements of rubato (suspension and aspiration).

4) In the area of fingering, he introduced a new system, one that called for the use of all fingers. He also insisted on the new numbering for the fingers from one to five as it appeared in 1593 in Girolamo Diruta's

treatise "Il Transilvano" and in the practice of the English virginal school almost more than one hundred 100 years before.

5) Coming now to articulation, Couperin was the first to introduce a technique for linking tones together in a precise way. He expressed the legato explicitly through the fingering.

6) In his table of ornaments he gives the smallest unit of phrasing the designation "*coulé.*" The suspension and aspiration ornaments should also be included among the phrasing devices.

7) In his work on methods Couperin provides the earliest reference to the musical memory and commentary concerning the way it should be developed.

8) Finally, Couperin revealed to the world the concept of the beautiful in keyboard performance.

Couperin's observations were at one time referred to as guides to the interpretation of his own works. Today they are helping not only to reproduce his creations, but to interpret other music of his time as well, for the means by which the French harpsichordists expressed their art constitute the content of his work.

3. German Treatises of the Eighteenth Century

German Treatises of the Eighteenth Century

A whole series of German works on methods appeared in the eighteen century, particularly in the second half of the century:
— the book of keyboard instruction by Friedrich Wilhelm Marpurg (1718-1795) entitled *Die Kunst das Klavier zu spielen von dem Musicus an der Spree* (Berlin, 1750), revised and expanded under the title *Anleitung zum Klavierspielen der schöneren Ausübung der heutigen Zeit gemäss entworfen* (Berlin, 1755);
— *Versuch über die wahre Art das Klavier zu spielen*, the treatise of Carl Philippe Emmanuel Bach (1714-1788) published in Berlin in 1753;
— *Der sich selbst informierende Klavierspieler* (Halle, 1765) by Friedrich Wiedeburg;
— the *Klavier-Schule* of G. S. Löhlein (Leipzig, 1765);
— and the Lehrnende *Klavierschule oder Anweisung zum Klavierspielen für Lehrer und Lehrnende* by Daniel Gottlob Türk (1750-1813) and the *Unterricht im Klavierspielen* by G. F. Wolf, both published in 1789, in Halle and Göttingen respectively.

The German methods for keyboard can be said to be distinguished by the following essential characteristics.

First, they constitute closed systems of knowledge based upon the practical keyboard performing art of the eighteenth century. Particularly worthy of note in the case of the works cited above is the precision with which they approach the study of the various means of expression; they include instructions concerning both proper use and proper execution of these devices. Unlike the French methods, the German manuals of instruction present a closed system of classifying the ornaments employed at the time and express the principles of fingering in the form of instructions.

The German works on keyboard method deal with the same range of problems as the French. Unlike the French, however, the German methods have been written for all of the old musical instruments — harpsichord, clavichord and the early forms of the hammerclavier (fortepiano), etc.

The first fortepiano made its appearance in 1711, but the age of the hammerclavier in fact opens only with the closing decades of the eighteenth century, when the instrument makers had perfected the essential form of the fortepiano.

The German treatises also stand out in consequence of another feature: Entire chapters have been devoted to the art of counterpoint, harmony, figured bass, free improvisation, accompaniment, the art of ornamentation, cadences and improvisation of fermatas.

The *Versuch über die wahre Art das Klavier zu spielen* by Carl Philipp Emmanuel Bach and the *Klavierschule...* of Daniel Gottlob Türk are the two most important works on methods to appear in the eighteenth century. These works introduce new ideas, new concepts and an entirely new dimension to the subject at hand here. Attention therefore will be turned to them for more detailed analysis.

Carl Philipp Emmanuel Bach:
Versuch über die wahre Art das Klavier zu spielen

C. P. E. Bach's *Versuch,* published in Berlin in 1753 (facsimile edition published in Leipzig in 1957), is a work of uncommon value for the musician because without doubt it contains something of the thinking of the great Johann Sebastian Bach. But even if the famous connection with the great polyphonist is disregarded, this work would still be assured of a place of honor in the literature on harpsichord methods. The first part, in particular, has remained of interest and relevant down to the present time. It treats the subjects of fingering, ornamentation and interpretation. Haydn, Beethoven, Czerny and Clementi, too, held Bach's *Versuch* in very high esteem. Haydn said of this work that it was the school of schools and would remain so for all time.

The second part is an essay on harmony, the art of the thorough bass, counterpoint, and the art of the "free fantasia," which were the subjects customarily covered in the methods manuals of the time. Attention will be turned here to the first part of the treatise without intending in any way to detract from the value of the second.

Bach's work appeared 36 years after Couperin's *L'Art de toucher le clavecin*, which had been written exclusively for the harpsichord. Bach wrote his treatise with reference to all three of the keyboard-stringed instruments in use at the time, namely, the harpsichord, clavichord and hammerclavier, the last of which was coming to play an increasingly important role during this century.

Quotations in this chapter have been taken directly from Bach's *Versuch*.

Bach organized the first part of his treatise into a foreword, an introduction and three chapters. The introduction can in turn be divided into four sections:

1) contemporary demands placed on the keyboard instrumentalist;
2) fundamental principles of keyboard performance (these appear as the titles of the three chapters of the treatise);
3) mistakes in execution; and
4) contemporary instruments.

Of interest in the foreword is the description of the role of the contemporary keyboard instrumentalist, which was very different from the way it is thought of today. To give the full picture here the entire paragraph on page 2 will be quoted:

> At the same time, however, who can not be aware of how many demands we make of the keyboard instrumentalist, or of the fact that we are not satisfied with our expectation that he delivers what, of course, we have every right to expect of every instrumentalist, namely, an ability to play a piece of music written for his instrument in accordance with the rules of good performance? We demand over and above this that the keyboard player also be able to improvise fantasias in every style imaginable and to work out any setting requested extemporaneously, but at the same time in accordance with the most rigorous rules of harmony and melody, to play in all keys with equal facility, to transpose instantly and cleanly from one key to another and sight-read any and all material placed in front of him, whether it has in fact been written for his instrument or not; that he have completely mastered thorough bass and execute it with discernment, frequently departing from the text, sometimes in many voices, sometimes in only a few, now in strict conformity with the requirements of harmony, now in the galant style, from both under-indicated and over-indicated figured basses, now from basses which might be either incorrectly figured or unfigured entirely; that he be able when necessary to extract this thorough bass from scores of many lines with unfigured or even pausing bass lines, when, as they will occasionally do, one of the other voices comes in to establish the basis for the harmony, and thereby enhance and reinforce the overall harmonization

and be able to do who knows what else in addition? He must then be prepared in many instances to satisfy the demands placed upon him on an unfamiliar instrument, no attention whatsoever having been given to determining whether it is a good instrument or a bad one, or to whether it is in proper condition or not, excuses being accepted in these cases only rarely. On the contrary, he can expect to hear these overbearing requests for improvisations without anyone's even bothering to see whether he is in the right frame of mind for it or not, and if he is not in the mood for it, with no effort being made to create or maintain the proper disposition by providing him with a decent instrument.

These tribulations notwithstanding, the clavier was enjoying universal popularity as an instrument.

In Bach's day, the structure referred to as "the art of keyboard performance" rested on three foundation principles. These principles were interlinked; unsupported by the other two, none could stand alone. These were correct fingering, correct ornamentation and correct performance. Inadequate, or incorrect, understanding of these factors has been the root of many shortcomings in keyboard performance.

Performance shortcomings which can be attributed to incorrect understanding of these principles could be categorized as follows:

1) the tone of the instrument lacks clarity, a natural simplicity and the desired cantabile quality;

2) bad hand position, which impairs flexibility, makes the hands stiff and leads to imprecision, lack of clarity, dryness and roughness in tone;

3) the want of the desirable cantabile quality in the long legato tones is compensated by the employment of a variety of figures.

It was for precisely these reasons that C. P. E. Bach placed emphasis in his introduction on the principle of the inseparability of technical development and performance. He insists that the capabilities of both hands, which will be essential in all musical situations, be developed equally and that good taste be cultivated in the student right from the very beginning. He should spend time listening to good singers. Most importantly, suggests Bach, he should listen to the performance of arias, which does contribute to the development of good performance skills by the student, but nothing, however, to the development of the fingers.

In addition to the demands placed on the keyboard instrumentalist, the governing principles and the shortcomings which he wants to remedy through adherence to certain rules, the characteristics of the individual keyboard instruments and comparisons between them are particularly important points raised in the introduction. Of the large number of different keyboard instruments of the day, the harpsichord and clavichord were the ones enjoying the greatest popularity.

The clavichord:

> When they are solid and well-built, the more recent fortepianos have many merits, this despite the fact that to master the touch requires a particularly concerted effort, something which is not without its difficulties. They give a good account of themselves as solo instruments and as an ensemble instrument when they are not overpowered by the other instruments. I am of the opinion, however, that, except for the fact that it has a weaker tone, a good clavichord will exhibit all the attractive qualities of the fortepiano, plus the capabilities of *bebung* (page 36).

In his reflections, Bach explains the execution of the *bebung* as follows: the clavichordist "imparts a vibrato to a long, affetuoso note by rocking, so to speak, the key with the finger which has depressed it" (page 36). This type of vibrato, which can be produced only on the clavichord, is one of the characteristics that gives this instrument its particular charm. The sign for vibrato is ⌢⋯⋯. In Bach's view, the good clavichord would be characterized by "an alluring tone which is clearly audible and carries well" (page 36), a keyboard range of C–e^3 and the production of tones which can be slightly varied with respect to both pitch and intensity. "The clavichord, therefore, is the instrument on which the keyboard instrumentalist may be most completely and accurately evaluated."[4]

The harpsichord, in Bach's view, should have a good tone over the entire range of the instrument and uniform quilling, that is, evenly balanced mechanics. The keys should not fall too deep, and the fingers should meet resistance from them and then be raised immediately back up again by the jacks. Both instruments must be properly tempered so they can be played in all 24 keys.

As far as the use of the harpsichord was concerned, Bach insisted in paragraph 15 that

> every good keyboard player would do well to have both a good harpsichord and a good clavichord so as to be able to play any piece on either instrument. The good clavichordist will be able to play the harpsichord equally well, but the reverse is not true. The clavichord should therefore be used to develop good performance skills and the harpsichord to bring the fingers up to their proper strength.

(With Couperin the advanced student would progress from the harpsichord with one manual to the harpsichord with two manuals to develop the necessary strength in the fingers.) Still another reason the keyboard instrumentalist should play both instruments consists in the fact that a player who plays the harpsichord exclusively will become accustomed to playing in only one timbre. The varied touch which a good clavichordist can develop will not come through.

What program of instruction did a teacher offer some 36 years later after Couperin?

He would

1) teach the fundamentals of music theory;
2) instruct the student in the different types of fingering;
3) drill the student in the execution of the different ornaments; and
4) start the student on the simpler pieces (without ornamentation) on the clavichord and then advance him to the harpsichord.

The pieces in the *Versuch* are arranged by degree of difficulty, which does increase rapidly. The course of instruction in methods proposed by Couperin and the one now suggested by C. P. E. Bach are identical in their essentials. In this connection a brief examination of the program of instruction offered by J. S. Bach follows. C. P. E. Bach recalls his father's approach to keyboard instruction: "My late father could look back on many successful experiments based upon this approach. He would introduce his students immediately to some of his more difficult pieces. So nobody should be intimidated by my pieces" (page 40). The pieces of moderate difficulty referred to here would include the two-part inventions and the short preludes, which were not as easily accessible as the compositions of C. P. E. Bach. "Work on the development of performance skills generally would be greatly benefitted and at the same time simplified by the simultaneous study of voice and by listening carefully to good singers" (page 39). Rameau was of the same opinion.

C. P. E. BACH ON THE PRINCIPLES OF GOOD TECHNIQUE

The discussion here will follow the outline presented in the Introduction.

The physical apparatus as a factor in performance:

1) posture
2) hand position
3) finger mechanics

4) motion in playing
5) relaxation of the locomotor apparatus

Before turning to individual points in detail, what follows is a reminder of some of the basic pointers Bach has to offer here, suggestions he holds to be of fundamental importance: If they are not followed, even the best of rules will remain of only potential benefit. These principles bear a striking resemblance to those which still form the basis of today's instructional methods. According to points 1, 2 and 5, one should be positioned at the midpoint of the keyboard so as to be able to reach both ends with equal ease. "...We should play with arched fingers and relaxed nerves" (page 42). The meaning of the last expression here is clear: Bach clearly is referring to relaxed "muscles." There is no objection to be raised here, of course, since it can be assumed that C. P. E. Bach had studied no anatomy.

> Stiffness is an impediment to all motion and particularly impairs the ability to extend and contract the palms quickly.... Those who play with extended fingers and rigid muscles will at the same time be inflicting upon themselves another critical disadvantage, in addition to the awkwardness this inevitably causes, namely, they will find the other fingers, because of their length, too far removed from the thumb.... This explains the fact that those who use the thumbs only rarely will in many instances play stiffly, whereas the player who uses them correctly could not even play this way if he wanted to (page 43).

These rules should still be observed today, of course, but the fact is that they are needlessly disregarded. Stiff, insufficiently relaxed hands and fingers impair all motions and work to the disadvantage of the performer, particularly when he must extend and contract the palms rapidly. These movements are of continual use in playing. It is absolutely essential that the palms and fingers remain relaxed and limber, particularly when it comes to passages which call for the extended spans or for using the fingers farthest removed (as opposed to those nearest) to strike closer-lying keys, to finger substitutions and, most importantly, to crossing the fingers and turning the thumbs. Leaps and long spans would constitute exceptions here: In these cases, of course, it is impossible to meet the requirement for arched fingers and relaxed muscles in view of the fact that, for an instant, it becomes necessary to tense both the palms and the fingers, that is, the entire musculature of the hand. This is learned in the course of practical keyboard instruction. Pertinent in this connection is Bach's discussion in paragraphs 10-12 on pp. 18-19, where he deals with the problem of thumb position. The thumb should be kept as close as possible to the palm; otherwise, this digit, the most important as far as Bach is concerned, is unable to perform its full range of functions. If the thumb is used only rarely in playing, this will cause stiffness in the hand, an effect, of course, which also works in the opposite direction. The use of the thumb gives the hand another digit; beyond that, it also enables the performer to relax his hands.

> He will find himself able to play the most difficult pieces in such a manner that the movement of his hands will be barely noticeable; most importantly, it will sound to the listener as though these pieces presented no difficulties. On the other hand, we will frequently see another play even the simplest of pieces unusually awkwardly and with much snorting and grimacing (page 43).

The theme of this passage is the functional efficiency of fingering. In the context of keyboard practice, "functional efficiency" refers to the purposeful use of the shortest, most direct movements in preference to less efficient motions. Purposeful motions are not only aesthetically pleasing, they also permit the pianist to make the most economical use of both his physical and mental energies. What conclusions can the educator now draw from this sampling of Bach's thinking on these points?

First, that Bach attaches great importance to insuring maximum relaxation and flexibility of the locomotor apparatus.

Second, one can conclude that he wanted to see the development of a technique in which the entire hand is brought together into a functional unit. Combined with the requirement that the fingers be arched, this provides the rounded hand looked for today.

Third, today one concurs with the view that to play with excessive and exaggerated movements is a bad habit. Bach places great emphasis on the fact that it also possible to play with restrained, disciplined movements.

In Chapter 1 of the *Versuch* one finds the most important principle governing the development of proper keyboard technique. It is a principle which will be found in all the familiar modern methods as well.

CHAPTER I: FINGERING

"Von der Finger-Setzung" is the modest title given to this lengthy chapter. The discussion here is characterized first and foremost by the fact that Bach does not really concern himself with any details of structure as

Couperin was inclined to do, but rather with general principles, on the basis of which the interpreter can then choose the fingering most appropriate for the widest range of compositions entirely on his own. It must be admitted that he achieved a high degree of success with this approach. Essentially, Bach proceeds here on the bases of the natural characteristics of the locomotor apparatus, the shape of the hands and the instrument, and the shape and configuration of the keyboard. These factors, then, will govern fingering. Bach himself writes as follows:

> [D]espite the endless variety of possible fingerings, a few good general examples and rules will nevertheless suffice to solve any problems which may arise and ... with diligent practice the use of the fingers ultimately becomes, and in fact must become, so mechanical that the student can freely begin to devote all his attention to the expression of more important things without having to concern himself any more with it.[2]

As far as C. P. E. Bach is concerned, the best fingering is the one which requires the least effort, correct fingering being an essential condition of optimum performance.

It can be seen that proper employment of the fingers is inseparably related to every aspect of the art of performance. Through incorrect fingering one loses more than can be replaced by any possible artistry or good taste.

This chapter is of the greatest importance from the point of view of what it represents for the development of fingering itself: Here once again, this time on German soil, appears the idea for the introduction of a new type of fingering and the suggestion that the keyboard musician use his thumbs. What in fact were the motivating factors in C. P. E. Bach's preoccupation with the idea of a new fingering system? His own words offer a highly original description of the situation at that time:

> Because every new idea calls for its own, virtually unique, fingering, present-day musical thinking, which represents a departure from the thinking of the past, has conceived a new system of fingering. Because they were more interested in harmony than in melody, our forefathers would ordinarily play in several voices. We will soon see that, given this mode of expression, wherein most passages can be executed in only one way and offer only limited possibilities for variation, each finger will be assigned, so to speak, its position. They therefore do not pose the same hazards as the melodic passages, what with the fact that in the case of the latter the fingering is much more arbitrary than is true of the former (pages 41, 42).

Bach laid down the basic rule that every new musical idea calls for its own fingering, which represented a major shift away from the thinking of the past.

Another factor in the development of the new fingering consisted in the tuning of the instrument:

> The instrument was formerly not as well tempered as it is today. As a consequence, the performer did not use all twenty-four keys as he does today. Neither, therefore, was there any great variety in the passages (page 42).

A third factor to be mentioned is the fact that, at least up to the time of Johann Sebastian Bach, the thumb was only very rarely employed. It was looked upon, rather, as something of an impediment to performance. Reflecting the prevailing view of the time, the protest was heard that "we would have too many fingers." J. S. Bach raised justifiable objections to this state of affairs. The possibility existed for composing in all keys. Structure was becoming increasingly more complex, and the need to bring in the thumb was obvious. One has only to recall Couperin's efforts in this connection. Interesting here is the passage in paragraph 7, page 5, which presents a picture of the situation prevailing when J. S. Bach was a young man.

> My late father told me that when he was a young man he used to hear great men who would use their thumbs only when the music required the hand to span an extended range of notes. Because he lived at a time of a gradual but marked shifting in musical taste, he was obliged to develop a much more comprehensive system of fingering, particularly so as to incorporate the thumbs, which, in addition to the other good services they render, are absolutely indispensable in the more difficult keys, and use them, so to speak, as Nature intended to be used. In so doing he elevated them at a stroke from their former uselessness to the position of principle finger.

The factors motivating the development of a new type of fingering, therefore, were the new mode of musical thinking, the better-tempered instrument of the time and a shortage of fingers.

Since C. P. E. Bach wanted to depart entirely from the old fingering, he elaborated an entirely new set of fingering principles. What is now available is a range of possible fingerings, from which the interpreter can choose the variations which best meet the requirements of a particular situation. The reference here, of course, is to particular technical situations which dictate a change in the position of the hand on the keyboard, situations in which the finger shortage is felt most keenly — in the execution of legato passages. These situations are encountered frequently, and Bach's principles apply first and foremost to this one problem. Over and beyond that, these principles can find highly productive application to compositions of the most diverse style and character. One find the answers Bach offers here scattered over ninety-nine paragraphs.

So what type of fingering facilitates the change in hand position required for legato playing? Bach has gone into this question in detail, and what follows is a summary of his thinking here under a number of points.

1. In those situations in which the five fingers fall short of the finger requirements, help may be attained by turning under the first finger, that is, the thumb, and crossing the fingers over the thumb coming in the opposite direction.

J. S. Bach and C. P. E. Bach have been incorrectly credited with the idea of turning the thumb. This had already appeared in the sixteenth century (J. Bermudo) in Spanish tablature manuals. This idea of the Spaniard Bermudo was unable to establish itself, however. J. S. Bach's contribution was now to rediscover this technique and adopt it in practice. And it is still in use today in the widest variety of passages and, of course, in scales as well. C. P. E. Bach's contribution was for the first time to incorporate his father's technique in the body of theory offered in the methods manuals of the time.

2. Crossing longer fingers over shorter, except for the thumbs.

As can be seen in following the development of fingering beyond this point, Chopin used this type of fingering both in his own playing and in instruction. Bach's, therefore, are the precursors of Chopin's ideas.

3. Striking adjacent keys with the same finger. Here it can be objected that it is not possible to produce a legato from two notes played with the same finger. This fine point of keyboard technique demands a high degree of skill and dexterity on the part of the performer. In Chopin's compositions one can find many passages in which two adjacent tones are linked together with the same finger (1,1, 5,5).

4. Substitution of fingers:

The silent, imperceptible substitution of fingers has become an integral component of modern-day fingering.

5. Bringing fingers separated from one another closer together; particularly important here is the idea of drawing the thumb toward the third, fourth and fifth fingers.

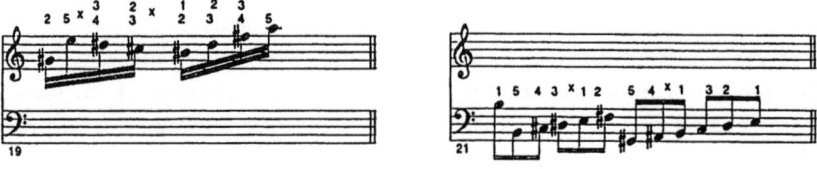

This point becomes important in connection with the interpretation of twentieth-century music.

6. Sliding the finger from the black keys onto the white keys. The example illustrates this movement for the fifth finger only. It is assumed the writer here accepted the possibility of executing this motion with other fingers as well. Many other examples from the body of Chopin literature come to mind in this connection, the slides of the fourth and first fingers in the preludes and sonatas.

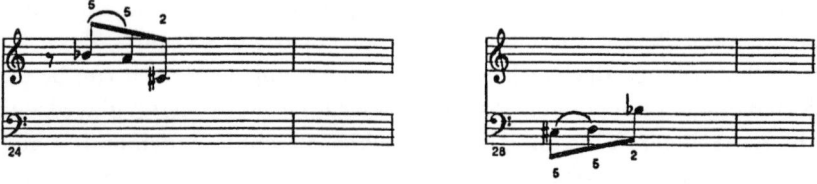

All the fingerings referred to here have constituted the alpha and omega for every keyboard instrument teacher down to the present day. By requiring the use of the thumb, Bach gave the hand not only another finger, but at the same time the code, so to speak, to the full range of fingering possibilities. In his "theory" Bach is anticipating thinking which will emerge in the course of the coming century (Chopin's *Theory of Fingering*).

Fingering must also always be devised so as to accommodate the individual peculiarities in hand development.

CHAPTER 2: ORNAMENTATION

This exhaustive chapter is organized into two parts. In the first part, Bach discusses the ornaments in general. In the second part one finds a very detailed description of the individual types of ornamentation (appoggiatura, shake, upper mordent [*Pralltriller*], turn, mordent, slide), the application of the ornaments in the musical literature and the technique of executing them.

The problem of ornamentation was one of the most important aspects of interpretation at this time, and it is therefore no coincidence that the technical exercises employed then began with ornaments (Bach, Couperin). The most comprehensive chapter in all the familiar methods manuals is invariably devoted to precisely this subject.

In the first paragraph of Chapter 2 C. P. E. Bach focuses the reader's attention on the essential questions of the importance, function and need for ornaments. Nobody questioned the need for ornaments in Bach's time. They were a universal presence in the music of the day, almost in every measure. They were necessary as connections between the notes and desirable for the life they imparted to the music.

It is also very important for the performing musician of today to acquaint himself with a number of other functions the ornaments perform. They will help him develop a deeper understanding of the eighteenth-century text.

What functions do the ornaments perform? They connect the tones and make a melody flow; they accentuate — underline, as it were — certain tones and passages in a composition; and they finalize the mood and comprehensive effect of the piece. Beyond these purely aesthetic functions, they perform a transformative function as well. They alter melody, rhythm and, most importantly, the harmonic components of a composition (dissonances and chords). Furthermore, they offer the interpreter opportunities to test the level of both his taste and his technical proficiency.

As musical devices, however, ornaments can be employed to two contrasting effects: They can ruin the best of compositions, while at the same time, the judicious introduction of embellishments can make a mediocre piece more interesting.

The more proficient performers would commonly add more

ornaments than were called for in the text. Bach's paragraph on this subject testifies to a state of affairs in which a certain freedom prevailed in the execution of ornaments. At the same time, however, a trend was gathering momentum which was increasingly hedging this generally established practice with more restrictive principles (Couperin's pronouncements, for example, and the texts of a number of French composers). Theirs was the legacy of the comprehensive notation (Marin Marais, De Caix d'Hervelois). The explanation for the liberties taken in the execution of embellishments and for such a negative attitude toward an exact musical notation is to be found in the practices of the harpsichordists of the day, who in the harpsichord parts would indicate all embellishments precisely, while contenting themselves in the others with only a few crosses (flute, violin). Rameau's triple concerti for violin or flute and harpsichord offer examples of this type of notation.

What thinking, now, did Bach leave on the subject of the employment of ornaments? The following are some of his ideas.

1) Critical to the choice of embellishments was the requirement that they alter neither the sense nor the expression of the composition.

2) Compositions which express feelings of grief and simplicity should be rendered with fewer embellishments than those expressing other emotions.

3) When it comes to the introduction of ornamentation, composers should always guard against excesses in the use of these devices. Each compares musical embellishments with the ornamentation employed in architecture:

> Above all, however, care must be taken to avoid excesses in the employment of our ornamentation. Embellishments should be regarded as decorations which, when added to excess, can mar the appearance of the most perfect structure, or as spices which can ruin the best dishes.[3]

4) Of the multitude of notes comprising a composition, only those should be embellished which require particular weight and emphasis:

> ...I would [otherwise] be committing the same error as an orator who tries to place a strong emphasis on each and every word; everything would sound the same and, as a consequence, lose in clarity (page 86).

5) Bach also writes that a composition

> in which all embellishments are indicated can for this reason be performed without undue concern, while in those in which few or none are

indicated [the performer] will be able to introduce them in conformity with established practice (page 81).

What did it mean for a performer to ornament a work in the conventional manner? What was the significance of the point at which an embellishment was to be inserted, or of the many other abilities? Bach would suggest here that the ear had to be cultivated to this point, specifically by listening to good music. It would behoove the keyboard performer above all to develop a solid grounding in harmony.

It is of no concern today that someone is going to be adding embellishments to a musical text. No teacher is interested in this question: no longer do performers embellish unfamiliar compositions in this way.

Bach next discusses the basic rules governing the execution of ornaments. One of the universally known rules can be stated as follows: The rhythmic value of an ornament must be subtracted from the note with which it is associated. In Couperin's day all musicians were bound to abide by this rule. C. P. E. Bach's rule on this point is:

> All embellishments indicated in small notes pertain to the following note; the preceding note, therefore, must never be denied its full value, while the following note will lose as much of its value as the small notes take from it. This observation increases in importance the more it is disregarded and the less it has been possible in the practice pieces to avoid at some points a separation between some of the small notes and the principal notes with which they are associated because of the space required for the mass of signs and markings to indicate fingering, ornamentation and expression (page 84).

Semantically, Bach's rule is identical to the rules referred to earlier. He was very likely forgetting about one exception, however — the so-called unaccented appoggiatura *(Nachschlag)*. The unaccented appoggiatura is an ornament which belongs not to the note which follows, but rather to the preceding note. By way of this exception the author of the *Versuch* confirms the familiar truth that in art there is no rule which has no exception.

A second, no less important, principle, one linked inextricably with the rule cited above and to which one must give particularly close attention, is formulated as follows:

> According to this rule . . . these small notes and not the principal note will be played together with the bass and the other voices (page 84).

That is, the ornamenting note, or notes in the case of the slide. Today this rule is frequently neglected, and not only by young players, but by the concert pianist as well. Tasteless renderings, in which the bass is delayed beyond the first note of the embellishment and sounded with the principal note, are common. There can be no doubt that in formulating these rules C. P. E. Bach was taking his guidance from the thinking of his father. He was, when all is said and done, his father's student.

Any discussion of the execution of ornaments must inevitably include consideration not only of the question of the proper deciphering of the sign, but of the matter of the dynamic proportionality between the ornamental notes and the principal notes of the text as well. Nowhere in the individual paragraphs of Bach's lengthy chapter can be found a straightforward answer to this question. The reason for this is perhaps to be sought in the fact that in the case of the harpsichord, the dynamics were by definition constant from one note to another, whereas the clavichord and hammerclavier player could take the possibility of variable dynamics for granted.

In observations scattered throughout this chapter can be found Bach's distinction between ornament and principal melody particularly clearly drawn where he declares that the dynamic volume of the trill will behave in conformity with both the context and the idea within which it occurs. Bach, therefore, plays his ornamented notes lightly and gracefully. When it comes to the performance of compositions of the old masters today, these performances will frequently be found to suffer not only from a deficient knowledge of the embellishments, but also, and primarily, from a failure to establish proper dynamic distinctions between embellishment and context. Trills will be executed loudly and heavily, in such a way as to create the impression of tedious, superfluous additions to the text, which, rather than embellishing a piece and adding to its appeal, detract from it.

Because certain ornaments will occur with equal frequency in both the bass and soprano voices, the student must practice the execution of these devices until he can play them perfectly, with both hands and with an equal degree of grace and dexterity. All imitations should be played carefully and thoroughly, the model copied down to the last detail in each voice. Solid mastery of the theme requires the left hand to be as well developed as the right:

> All imitations, moreover, must be reproduced down to the smallest detail. The left hand, therefore, should practice embellishments until it can imitate proficiently, for embellishments which lose in charm

through poor execution would otherwise best be omitted altogether.

Certain practical conclusions can be drawn from the last sentence. If a choice is allowed between a range of possible executions of an ornament or ornaments, or between different editions of the same composition, and if principles of style are taken into account as they apply to the performance of the composition, it will be better to choose the simplest version if it is certain that the performer will not be able render a more difficult version appropriately (that is, at the proper tempo).

In the second part of the first chapter, C. P. E. Bach introduces the individual groups of embellishments:

1) appoggiaturas (long and short)
2) trills
3) inverted mordents *(Pralltriller)*
4) turns
5) mordents
6) double appoggiatura
7) slide

C. P. E. Bach describes these embellishments in great detail. With the exception of the unaccented appoggiatura *(Nachschlag)*, he covers all ornaments which were to be found in the musical literature of the day. The selection was then supported with some of the most important examples of each ornament accompanied by instructions for proper execution. These can be found in the instructional keyboard literature.

Before looking at the individual embellishments themselves, it would be useful first to introduce a table J. S. Bach wrote out in these ornaments. This is important because it gives a basis for comparing the father with the son and, furthermore, because it contains material which every pianist and every music educator should be required to master. The ornaments are included in a book J. S. Bach intended for his oldest son, Wilhelm Friedemann Bach, which carries the title *Klavierbüchlein für W. Fr. Bach.*

The table on the following page includes only a small number of models (13). In his chapter on the subject, C. P. E. Bach includes a substantially larger number of embellishments together with detailed discussions of them. Between J. S. Bach and his son can be seen no essential differences in the execution they prescribe for the individual embellishments.

J. S. Bach's Ornament Table

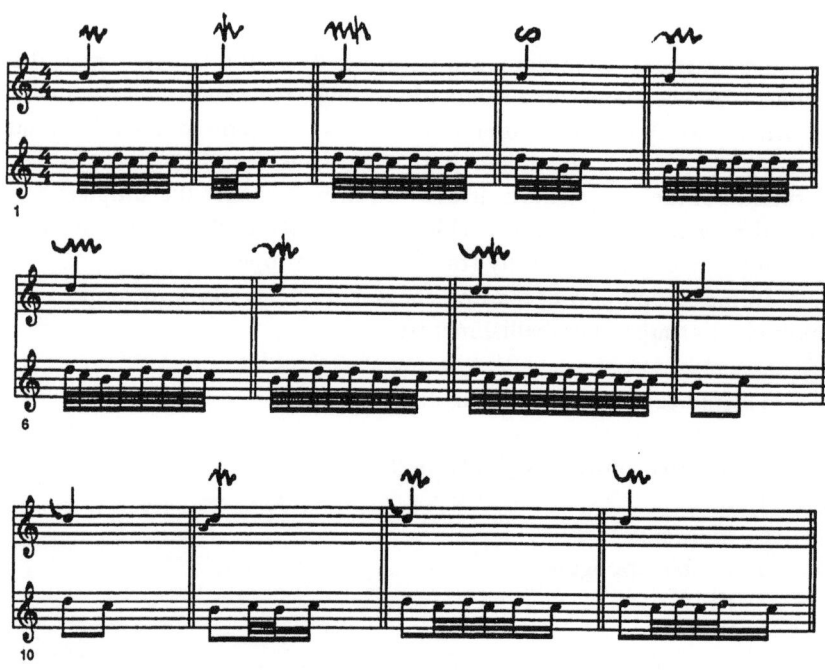

Ornament group 1: Trills

C. P. E. Bach distinguishes between four types of trills:

a) the standard trill
b) "ascending" trill (beginning from the upper second of the trilling note)
c) "descending" trill (beginning from lower second of the main note)
d) the half trill, referred to as the *Pralltriller* (inverted mordent).

The standard trill is notated differently:

This trill always begins a second above the principal note. The standard trill will occasionally be followed by a suffix; that is, two small ascending tones will be appended at the end. The suffix is in some instances written out in notes, while indicated in others by an alteration of the sign: ᴀᴀᴧ

The trill will have a suffix in the following cases:

1) when the sign for a trill appears over a long note;
2) when the trill is followed by a leap; and
3) when an ascending second follows on the trill line.

The suffix added to a trill must be played in the same tempo as the trill itself (unlike Couperin's slight deviation from the tempo, that is, an acceleration). If the piece is to be played at a rapid tempo, Bach suggests that the trill be replaced by an appoggiatura. Although it is only rarely followed, this advice is just as valuable today as it was when Bach first offered it.

In electing the trill to be employed, care must be taken to preserve the purity of the harmony and maintain proper voice leading. In present-day practice, however, this observation no longer finds application.

A trill must be executed with expression and rapidly. It can be played more slowly in the slower pieces. The dynamics of the trill should conform to both the context and the idea within which it occurs.

The ascending trill in J. S. Bach's embellishment table can be found under No. 5. Father and son execute this trill identically. C. P. E. Bach offers three possible notations:

J. S. Bach shows the descending trill as No. 6. C. P. E. Bach gives two notations, although neither indicates an execution differing in any way from that prescribed by his father.

The short trill consists of four notes. In C. P. E. Bach's discussion it carries the notation of the inverted mordent *(Pralltriller)*. The example shows the notation and the corresponding execution of this ornament. C. P. E. Bach explains that the inverted mordent must be played very rapidly, and as the note values (64) in the notation indicate, expressively and not excessively loudly. The performer who fails to follow this prescription will encounter substantial difficulty.

Ornament group 2: The mordents

To this ornament the author devotes an entire section, four pages and some 30 examples! This embellishment does not belong to the trills, as it had been treated heretofore. The example illustrates both the notation and the corresponding execution. Bach distinguishes three types of mordents: the long mordent (a), the short mordent (b) and the very short mordent (c). The short mordent is the embellishment used most frequently in the bass and is indicated by the sign ⟋⟍.

The discussion of the execution of the very short mordent is based upon Bach's own description. There is a particular execution of the mordent which is employed when this embellishment must be very short:

> Of the two notes struck, only the upper note is held; the other is released immediately. There is nothing objectionable about this execution, provided, of course, that this device is employed less frequently than the other mordents. It is played abruptly, that is, in unslurred passages only.

There are many interpreters and teachers who are unfamiliar with this type of mordent. It is used less frequently than the other mordents, in most instances in passages in which it is not connected with the preceding note, that is, at the beginning of a phrase or following a pause.

Ornament group 3: The turn

As of the middle of the eighteenth century the turn had yet to be associated with a specific sign. C. P. E. Bach did indeed replace the relatively expressionless ∼ sign, which is found in J. S. Bach's ornament table, with the symbol ∾ ; this sign, however, would be written differently: sometimes vertically, sometimes horizontally. C. P. E. Bach, of course, clearly pronounced himself in favor of the horizontally written sign, which is better from the purely graphic point of view. As can be seen from example 1, the execution of the turn will be dictated by the tempo of the piece.

With example 2 Bach illustrates the execution of a combination ornament — the turn combined with a long appoggiatura and an inverted mordent.

Ornament group 4: The appoggiaturas

C. P. E. Bach distinguishes two types of appoggiatura: the short (unvariable) appoggiatura and the long (variable) appoggiatura.

The appoggiaturas are written in small notes, which will either have different values or be written in very short values (8-32). The short, unvariable, appoggiatura most frequently precedes notes with short values. It will have one, two or three flags and be executed so rapidly that the following note loses none of its value.

The long, variable, appoggiatura, in Bach's view, should be given the rhythmical value indicated by the notation in which it is written. The variable appoggiaturas take half the rhythmical value of a following principal note of double length. From a following note of triple length they take two-thirds of the value. Most important here is C. P. E. Bach's prescription that all appoggiaturas must be executed more loudly than the principal note and are joined to it, whether a slur is indicated or not.

The appoggiaturas are long (variable), which indicates an adagio tempo.

Looking, now, at the notation for the two types of appoggiaturas, it can be seen that the differences between them are not substantial. The small note with a diagonal stroke through the flag ♪ which today indicates only the short appoggiatura, was not yet employed in Bach's day. Small notes were used to notate both types of appoggiatura at that time. Bach does indeed say that appoggiaturas will ordinarily be notated in small rhythmical values, but at the same time he refers to the eighths as well, which were also used to indicate the long appoggiatura. Today this sign gives rise to doubts and ambiguities. The author resolves these questions only partially and offers prescriptions referring to particular examples.

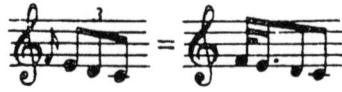

Appoggiaturas which precede triplets should be played very quickly so as not to alter the rhythm of the triplet.

Bach's thinking on the subject of ornamentation of all types requires respect, particularly when one comes to works which date from his time. The authority of the "father of keyboard pedagogy" remains undisputed. It would suffice in this regard to mention only the examples of commentaries included in the Polish edition of Chopin's works which deal with the subject of ornamentation and which will be found to follow the thinking of C. P. E. Bach (*Complete Works*, Paderewski, Bronarski and Turczyński, eds., publ. PWM).

CHAPTER 3: PERFORMANCE

The third and last chapter of the first part of Bach's essay on method does not cover its territory as extensively as do the first two chapters. Bach concentrates his attention here on the essential nature of keyboard performance itself and on the conditions which govern the performer's capacity for artistically correct performance at the keyboard. The individual paragraphs treat the questions of dynamics, tempo, touch, the technique of making the instrument "sing," and imprecision in the execution of the musical notation. The last paragraph presents some interesting thinking, which, however subtly, applies the aesthetic-artistic theory of affect to creative performance on the part of the interpreter, although Bach says nothing at all about the theory itself. Not only this chapter, but virtually the entire first part of Bach's essay can be said to exhibit still another characteristic feature, namely, that, in a certain sense, it can be described as constituting a negative method. That is to say, it would appear that Bach wanted to elucidate certain phenomena with reference not to positive, but rather, by and large, to negative examples. He illustrates a phenomenon on the basis of how something should *not* be done and what is incorrect, from which, however, it is in fact possible to develop a clear view of the desired objective as a whole. Bach's approach and his thinking in this regard is valued, because to the artistically cultivated reader of today they offer wise and insightful criticism and at the same time guide one in the direction of positive development, positive attributes.

If his last chapter is placed within the context of what has been referred to as the negativity of Bach's approach, one cannot fail to take account of his reflections on the larger theme of what it is that degrades performance quality. One negative phenomenon to be encountered in keyboard practice consists in the misuse of an ability to achieve great finger velocity at the expense of an ability to arouse the emotions and, accordingly, in what would have to be termed an abuse of the positive characteristics of the keyboard instrument. Of the three instruments for which Bach wrote his *Essay,* the hammerclavier would be the one most nearly corresponding to the potentialities of high-velocity execution.

This is unquestionably an erroneous preconception, as though the forte of a keyboard performer consisted in velocity pure and simple. The fact is, however, that a performer may have the nimblest of fingers, be proficient in the execution of single and double trills, master the intricacies of fingering, be able to play at sight no matter how many key changes a piece may confront him with and to transpose extemporaneously without the slightest difficulty, play tenths, and even twelfths, execute runs and crossovers of every conceivable variety and shine in any number of other aspects of keyboard performance and still not prove himself a lucid, pleasing, moving instrumentalist. Experience has shown us more often than not that though such performers be true technicians and skillful professional players possessing all these qualifications without exception, that while they may astound the faculties with their purely technical prowess at the keyboard, they will nevertheless remain incapable of reaching the soul and touching the sensibilities of their listeners. They dazzle the ear, but give it no pleasure; they stun the mind, but cannot satisfy it.

Returning to the subject at hand: What, for Bach, constituted the essence of good performance?

Good performance rests upon "the ability through singing or playing to sensitize the ear and make it conscious of the true content and emotion of musical ideas."[4] Musical performance should therefore be understood to consist in clearly and accurately conveying the musical truth embodied in the text.

And what, according to Bach, are the instrumentalities of performance? He refers to these as the "subject matter" of performance and enumerates them as follows:

1) the loudness and softness of tones and the intensity of the attack employed (what is referred to today as dynamics);

2) the velocity of execution (tempo);

3) the range of touches employed: legato, staccato, arpeggiation, and *Bebung* (touches varying according to articulation); and

4) the holding of tones, retardation and acceleration (variations in tempo, agogics).

It is interesting to note here that among the instrumentalities of performance Bach does not include devices which he discusses toward the end of his chapter, phrasing, for example, the emotion essential to good playing and the rhythmic precision required. This is probably because he considered these components of performance to rest upon the four categories of instrumentality enumerated above, factors which establish the general foundation for all others.

Depending on the combinations in which the performer employs these devices and the interaction between them, the listener will experience of higher or poorer quality.

> Good performance, therefore, will be recognized immediately when the listener hears all notes, together with the embellishments associated with them, executed in correct time, with the proper dynamics, and produced with facility by a touch appropriate to the true content of the composition.

Poor performance is a result of failure to employ these devices altogether, or to employ them correctly.

Still another factor contributing to good performance, in Bach's view, consists in "listening to the first-rate musicians." Bach offers this suggestion twice in his introduction and then once again in the chapter on performance itself.

In his discussion of tempo, Bach turns his attention to the question of how the performer is to establish the appropriate tempo for a composition. Because this important aspect of performance was ordinarily not reflected in the musical notation, the problem of tempo was a much discussed question of the time. The interpreter was expected to be able to take account of a multitude of factors and then on this basis to arrive at a correct decision concerning the tempo appropriate for a piece. (J. S. Bach was an exception in this respect. In some places he does include tempo markings in his compositions, for which practice he was also roundly derided by contemporaries.) Thus the process involved in deciding upon an appropriate tempo was a much more creative process than it is now, particularly when one finds precise metronome settings indicated in the text. Bach's practical suggestions concerning tempo were valid and useful for his time. Attention is given to his observations here because they can still be very helpful in elucidating and interpreting the detailed aspects of tempo, despite the fact that metronomes are available today.

And how should one establish the type of tempo appropriate for a piece? "The sprightliness of the allegro will generally be expressed by detached, staccato small value notes, the tenderness of the adagio in the more measured, slurred notes." C. P. E. Bach reminds the performer that the distinctions between these two tempi must always be maintained, even in those cases in which the tempo is not specifically indicated in the text. Deficient performance will in most instances result from inadequate understanding of the contrasts involved here. Bach's observations have lost none of their relevance over the years, particularly given the fact that he directs them to what he sees as the most frequent source of error in execution: "In some parts the fault most frequently heard in performance will be the tendency to play the adagios too fast and the allegros too slowly."

In determining the appropriate tempo for a piece, however, the performer must still deal with the problem of the precise speed at which it is to be played once the basic tempo has been decided upon ("speed," that is, in the sense of the precise setting one would use on today's metronome). According to Bach, the speed of execution can be fine-tuned on the basis of

1) the content of the piece overall;
2) the familiar Italian markings (if these have been included in the text); and, particularly,
3) the smallest rhythm values and the quickest figures.

Particular attention should be called to the last point. It is one with which even some educators are unfamiliar.

In his introduction Bach refers once again to the deficiencies most frequently heard in the touch employed in his time. These are errors which can be described in terms of two categories: the "sticky" touch and the overly abbreviated touch.

Bach sees the cause of these errors to lie in the fact that the performers who play this way are not giving the notes their proper rhythmic value; that is, the note values are being extended or abbreviated where they should not be.

The following is a look at the guidance Bach offers when it comes to the fine points of executing staccato notes, instructions which for the time are unusually precise. The detached notes can be played in a variety of ways; everything will depend on the value of the notes indicated, whether the basic tempo is fast or slow, and the dynamics of a particular passage, that is, whether it is to be played forte or piano. These notes will always be shortened by a little more than half their indicated value.

a)    b)

Bach would approach both these passages differently from Couperin, and in fact play them in precisely the opposite way, that is, the way they would be performed today. "In other instances the notes will be played such that the accent comes at the beginning of a slur." The dynamics of detail are dealt with here, that is, the dynamics of individual notes, and then with the accentuation of these notes, a point which D. G. Türk would later treat more thoroughly. The last note of the slur in passage b must be shortened "by raising the finger immediately." This describes the release employed today. Observe the slight difference in the notation here: The notation used in passage b calls for a staccato execution at the end of the slur. These notes will therefore be released in the manner referred to today as the "drop-lift." This was not the practice in Couperin's day. The slur with staccato at that time indicated the opposite articulation and called for the notes to be played in a different rhythm. This has already been examined in some detail in the discussion of Couperin's *L'Art de toucher le clavecin*, specifically in the closing section. To Bach's way of thinking, both versions could be employed to effect on either the clavichord or the harpsichord. Hence it followed that individual notes could indeed be accentuated (minidynamics) on the harpsichord, which would be important from the point of view of both the expression with which a piece is performed and the phrasing employed (at least when it comes to the extremely brief periods of time involved here). Bach would otherwise have given no attention to the "loudness and softness of notes."

On the subject of the dynamics of individual notes, attention should be called to still another one of Bach's observations, one which becomes extremely important as applied to the present-day approach to the playing of dissonances: Dissonances should be played more loudly than consonances, the former expressing a certain emotional tension, the latter then resolving it.

The discussion to this point has focused on the fundamental aspects of performance. Attention now will be turned to some secondary aspects associated with them. Bach discusses them in the closing paragraphs of his chapter on performance.

The period spanning the sixteenth to eighteenth centuries saw the effort to develop a cantabile style of rendering the melody line remain a persistent problem in the performance aesthetics of the time, this type of execution being by no means an easy thing on an instrument with an inability to prolong tones or to allow continuous increases and decreases in volume. And the problem of the cantabile tone has remained a problem to the present day. When thinking of the instruments available today, and then looking back at the stringed keyboard instruments used in Bach's time, one cannot but admire his solution of the problem. Vocalists and other instrumentalists would not know these shortcomings. Bach overcame them with embellishments. And when it came to this fine point, he insisted that the performer play all embellishments with a full, round tone so as to create in the listener the impression that he was hearing the unadorned main notes only and not any auxiliary notes, that is, the embellishments. Bach's solution comprehends a method the performer can use relatively effectively to deal with this problem.

As has been observed, Bach did not include any discussion of the theory of affect in his chapter on performance, but the theses of this theory can be identified in a number of considerations. Today's listener, of course, cannot know whether the performers of Bach's time emotionally experienced the ideas expressed in the compositions they played, and if they did, how and to what degree. The view has developed over the course of the centuries that the playing in Bach's time was dry and unagogic. One can respond in terms that will make it sufficiently clear that the playing of this period was indeed expressive and give a good idea of just how expressive the playing of the German musicians was.

> Now a musician cannot move others unless he himself is moved. He must therefore of necessity be able to feel all the emotions he wants to arouse in his listeners. He conveys his own feelings and emotions to them and in so doing stirs similar responses in them, responses stimulated both by the emotion they observe in the performer and by what they hear. This would also be the case with the passionate, lighthearted and other types of passages, where he must then arouse in himself the feelings appropriate here.[5]

Bach did not content himself with only the emotional component of performance, that is, with the performer's intuition, his ability to comprehend and then effectively convey the emotional content of a piece to his listeners. The piece must also be thoroughly studied.

> It is of course only rarely possible to convey the true content and emotion of a piece on a first reading. Even the most practiced orchestras will frequently require more than one rehearsal of pieces which, to judge only from the notes, are very easy.

One of the observations on instruction Bach offers in his concluding chapter applies to educators. Teachers, he insists, should not train their students like birds:

They must be able to play with a freedom which rules out all that is slavish and mechanical. The performer must play from the soul, not like a trained bird.

SUMMARY

In the evolution of the new keyboard methods, C. P. E. Bach stands as a pioneering figure. The thinking embodied in his system looks neither to the music of earlier periods nor to the music of his father. Of the old music one has a complete picture and an adequate store of information. As against his contemporaries—Haydn and Mozart—Bach and his method, and the principles embodied in this method, are of crucial significance. A considerable number of his instructions have been followed down to the present day. Others were already being superseded or modified to some extent in Bach's own time, the period of Vienna Classicism (D. G. Türk).

What now follows is a point by point summary, indicating what is new with Bach and at the same time comparing C. P. E. Bach with François Couperin.

First of all, Bach developed his *principles of performance* not only for the harpsichord, but also for the other two instruments of his time, the clavichord and the hammerclavier.

As far as *method* is concerned, Bach's approach parallels Couperin's but for some minor exceptions. Not as many technical patterns in Bach will be found, however.

Both authors begin their *courses of instruction* in keyboard playing on the instrument in the same manner, specifically, on the light keyboard, Bach on the clavichord.

In the area of *technique,* Bach recommends that the player maintain proper posture at the instrument, a "rational" posture which will permit smooth, efficient movement. Here he is restating the principle outlined by Couperin.

Bach is the first to speak of the importance of *purposeful motion.* This is probably the instruction of his father speaking. In advancing this idea, Bach gave impetus to the development of the theory and teaching of hand mechanics *(Motorik),* which emerged as an important interest at the beginning of the twentieth century.

Bach refers for the first time to a *hand position* in which the fingers are arched, and to the closed palm configuration preferred today.

Bach recognized the difference in *touch* between instruments, that the harpsichord requires one, the clavichord another. From this understanding emerges his suggestion that the harpsichord be used for technical purposes, the clavichord for performance.

Bach was the first to explain the type of touch referred to as "vibrato" *(Bebung)*.

When it comes to basic rules governing the execution of *ornaments*, Couperin and Bach may be found in agreement. With one exception, Bach brought together and classified all ornaments employed in his time.

Bach had introduced the inverted mordent *(Pralltriller)* and short appoggiatura as new ornaments, but he did not resolve the problem of the notation to be used for the two types of appoggiaturas.

In Bach's method one finds the first reference to a *dynamic* emphasis of dissonances and the establishment of distinctions between embellishments and the musical context in which they are embedded. Couperin developed no ideas on dynamics because he played only the harpsichord.

Bach established rules governing *fingering* to be employed in particular technical situations. He established a theoretical basis of the requirement for the use of the thumb and offered a systematized statement of his thinking on the problem of playing with too few fingers.

Bach elaborated a hierarchy of performance devices.

In contrast to Couperin, Bach developed a form of release used today referred to as the "drop-lift."

Bach insisted that the emotional and rational were equally important components of performance.

Finally, Bach identified himself with Couperin's critical observations concerning the divergence between musical text as written by the composer and performance.

Daniel Gottlob Türk: *Klavierschule oder Anweisung zum Klavierspielen für Lehrer und Lehrnende*

By the end of the eighteenth century Türk's *Klavierschule* had established itself as both the most widely used and the most comprehensive (at 374 pages) "tutor" for the keyboard. It covered all problems of the Baroque period. One finds in this manual a well-organized presentation of all postulates of what we can refer to as the "old" methods in the best sense of this term. As used here this term refers to instructional literature contained in manuals appearing from the fifteenth century (when we see the appearance of the first manuals of keyboard instruction) up to the end of the eighteenth century. Türk's *Klavierschule* appeared in many editions. For purposes of the discussion here reference will be made to the last, enlarged, edition—the original, which was published in Vienna in 1798 and, unlike the previous edition of 1789, had already been transposed to the violin clef.

The introduction and the organization of the first chapter of Türk's *Klavierschule* call to mind C. P. E. Bach's *Versuch*. In his introduction Türk discusses the most important types of keyboard instruments, the characteristics of a good keyboard and a good teacher, together with a number of introductory topics. His discussion of performance technique offers nothing new, particularly concerning his treatment of rules governing hand position and posture at the instrument and the motor aspect of keyboard playing. Here Türk is simply summarizing the thinking of his predecessors. For this reason no further attention will be paid to the introduction to the *Klavierschule*.

CHAPTER I: FUNDAMENTALS

In the six lengthy sections of his first chapter Türk discusses the fundamentals of score reading, accompaniment, notation (for the keys C, F, and G), harmony, expression markings, time, tempo, rhythm, and other topics. For purposes of the present discussion the first chapter will be disregarded, except for Section 4, paragraphs 53–68, where for the first time in the history of keyboard instructional literature appears an extended analysis of time, and Section 5, where Türk discusses tempo (movement).

Up to this point, no writer on keyboard method had given so much attention to time or attached so much importance to it. Türk in fact held that it was more important to "stay in time" than to strive for perfection from the point of view of technical proficiency. At the time Türk was writing his book on methods, all Europe was playing the music of Haydn and Mozart. This explains the emphasis he placed on playing in time. One of the most important characteristics of a proper interpretation of compositions of the Vienna classical composers was regularity in the "pulse" of the performance. Accentuation of the metrically heavy beats is only one way to keep in time. Türk insists that each detail of the notation must be studied thoroughly (the accents properly assigned) and the proper balance maintained between the smallest rhythmical values. This is a requirement he introduces in the very first "Exercises in Time."

3. GERMAN TREATISES

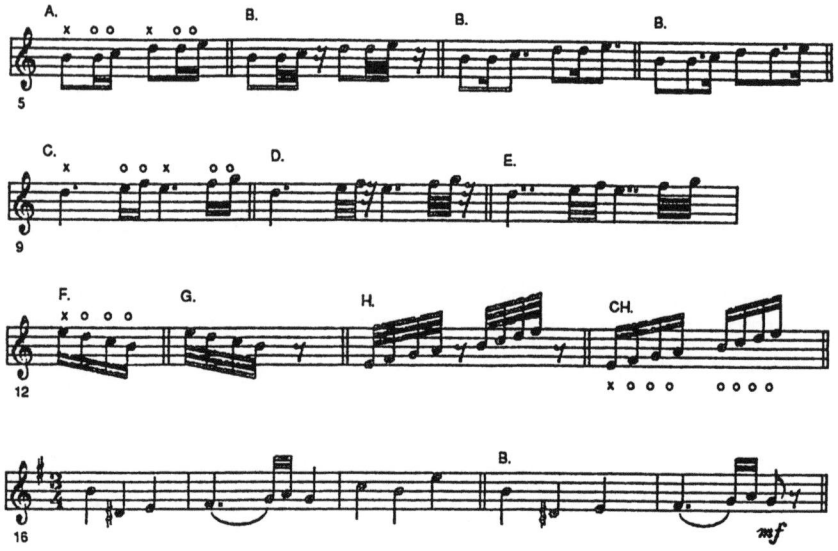

Examples b, d, e, g and h represent the notes in examples a, c, f and ch played with improperly allocated time values. The crosses here indicate the accented, the circles the unaccented notes. Proper accentuation and its opposite are among the devices which help the performer play in precise time. At the same time Türk emphasizes the importance of maintaining the proper evenness between the smallest rhythmic values.

When Türk speaks of time, one can see from his observations in this regard that it is rhythm and tempo he has in mind.

What melodic devices does Türk offer to help the student develop a good sense of time (what we would refer to today as a "feel for rhythm")?

In addition to the technique of accenting the beat, which presumes thorough understanding of the note values, Türk here reintroduces the device, which had been employed earlier but by Türk's time forgotten, of giving the time. This method had already been known in the Spanish theoretical literature of the sixteenth century, and it appears once again in a number of instructional manuals in the twentieth century (Bartók). Türk's teaching technique has found application in keyboard instruction down to the present today, a technique which consists in teacher and student playing together.

> A beginner should play only examples consisting of notes of equal value and then proceed gradually to examples with notes of varying value (first with one hand, later with both hands).

This approach helps the student develop an ability to maintain precise note values. Counting while playing is another device Türk discusses, but one which poses considerable difficulty for the beginner, who in this situation is required to give attention to both aspects of playing simultaneously. From time to time the teacher should therefore relieve the student, who then has to concern himself with only the counting.

Beating time with the foot is a technique other instrumentalists frequently use to enforce regularity in time and rhythm. When it comes to the keyboard players, however, to beat time lightly with the foot is not as reliable an aid as it may be in the case of other instruments because of the fact that irregular passages, in which the rhythm may vary, can be encountered in both hands. Türk's contribution consists in his observation that the performer can also keep proper time in his playing by dividing the measure mechanically and then accenting the beats accordingly. Simple measures, what are referred to as duple and triple time, would have the accent on the first, or heavy, beat.

a)   b)

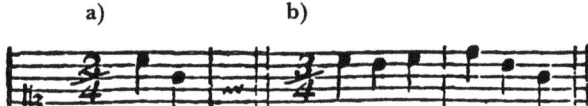

Türk was highly competent and experienced in the practical aspects of keyboard performance and was striving more in the direction of imparting practical knowledge than of restating a theory of time. He defined "playing in time" as the "proper organization of a certain number of notes which are to be played within a particular interval of time" (page 57, paragraph 53). The tempo indicated will determine the length of this time interval or how fast the beat should be.

Regarding tempo, Türk devotes himself to a highly detailed analysis of tempi and divides them into four main categories. He attempts to establish tempo precisely and in his work adopts Quantz's method of determining tempo with reference to the human pulse. Maelzel's metronome did not yet exist at this point. At *Allegro assai* in 4/4 time, one beat of a healthy pulse would correspond to a half note, to a quarter note with an indication of *Allegretto* and in *Adagio* or *Larghetto* to an eighth note.

This method still does not establish tempo with precision. Another device, similar to the Quantz method, which Türk employed to set a tempo more precisely was the pocket watch, which ticked at an average rate, namely 260–280 ticks per minute. The ticking of the pocket watch thus became a reference against which the rate of the beat could be established. Each quarter-beat at *Allegro assai* (in 2/4 time), for example, would correspond to two ticks of the clock, four ticks at *Allegretto* and eight ticks at *Allegro assai* in 4/4 time; that is, one eighth note would be played for each tick of the clock. The other note and beat values can then be established with reference to these tempi. Türk, of course, was well aware of the fact that, ultimately, these aids were inadequate. And in paragraph 75 he calls for someone to develop a general-purpose device which would be more precise than that available at the time.

When it came to tempo, Türk required discipline. It is the responsibility of the teacher to correct and eliminate errors which frequently occur in keyboard execution (acceleration, increases and decreases in tempo). And the teacher bears the blame if he is unable to maintain a tempo established at the beginning through to the last note of a piece.

CHAPTER 2: FINGERING

The lengthy second chapter is devoted to problems in the area of fingering. Türk offers no new ideas whatsoever here. He builds on the same principles which C. P. E. Bach laid down. In paragraph 2 on page 97 Türk states the following:

> Generally speaking, the fingering which is most convenient, or which requires the least motion of the fingers, will be the best.... [A fingering] whose chief objectives are not convenience and at the same time gracefulness in execution is inappropriate and, accordingly, a bad one.

Türk laid down the following fingering rules, which can stand as a summary of the rules which governed fingering in the eighteenth century.

1) Place the thumb (a) behind the black key or (b) ahead of the black key.

2) Place the thumb under the second, third and fourth fingers.

3) Bring the second, third and fourth fingers over the thumb.

4) Use the thumb and little finger on the black keys only in exceptional situations.

5) Do not use the same finger twice in succession, unless there is a pause between the tones or the repeated use of one finger does not break up the phrase.

6) Use the fingers in their natural sequence.

7) In executing jumps and playing broad intervals, leave out as many fingers as there are keys.

8) The repetition of a tone (at rapid tempos) requires an alternation of fingers.

9) Prolonged tones (in legato passages) will (in most instances) require a finger substitution following the attack.

The remaining sections of this chapter will be disregarded to avoid repetition of previous discussion (fingering for continuous, stepwise single-voice runs, scales, intervals played with one hand, three- and four-voice passages and associated jumps).

CHAPTERS 3 AND 4: ORNAMENTATION

The second half of the century saw major changes in ornament notation. New markings made their appearance, while the established markings began to be interpreted in new ways. When it came to the execution of ornaments, C. P. E. Bach and Couperin could not offer satisfaction. The instructions contained in these works were undoubtedly the deciding guidelines as compared with the offerings of contemporaries, and, as has been pointed out above, most of these instructions will still be taken into account today, although at the end of the century some were either elaborated or modified. What elevates Türk's work above the other systems, including even C. P. E. Bach's work, is the way he presents his material, the style of his notation, his explanations of the various embellishments and the basic organization of the work itself. C. P. E. Bach had omitted the unaccented appoggiatura *(Nachschlag)* and remained unclear in his notation and discussion of the execution of the short and long appoggiaturas. Türk, on the other hand, devotes his entire third chapter to these questions. Here he tries to clear up the confusion which had grown up around the ornaments due to the frequently conflicting views of the experts. The other ornaments are discussed in Chapter 4. To give the reader a better idea of the problems he deals with, an outline is offered below of the discussion contained in the third and fourth chapters of Türk's work.

Chapter 3. Appoggiaturas: Accented and unaccented [*Vorschlag* and *Nachschlag*]
1. General remarks on appoggiaturas
2. Variable appoggiaturas
3. Invariable appoggiaturas
   — the short, invariable appoggiatura
   — the short, ambiguous appoggiatura
4. The unaccented appoggiatura

Chapter 4. The essential ornaments
1. General remarks on ornamentation
2. Ornaments indicated by small notes
   — the double appoggiatura [*Anschlag*]
   — turn [*Doppelschlag*]
   — slide [*Schleifer*]
3. Essential ornaments indicated by markings
   — general remarks on trills
   — trill with the ending (suffix)
   — trill without any ending
   — descending trill
   — ascending trill
   — upper mordent [*Pralltriller*]
   — mordents
   — acciaccaturas
   — turn
4. Combined and other ornaments (included among the familiar "other" ornaments is the "vibrato" [*Bebung*])

Missing from Türk's original text, which has been taken as a guide here, are pages 177–226 (that is, Sections 2, 3 and 4 of Chapter 3 and Sections 1 and 2 of Chapter 4). Missing from Chapter 4 as well are the first three headings in Section 3 and the last heading in Section 4.

Concentration will be made here on only the most important points in this work. In Türk is found first of all an important difference in the notation employed for the short and long appoggiaturas. A note with a slash through the flag and stem is introduced as new notation indicating a short appoggiatura ♪. Türk includes this new device in the second edition of his *Klavierschule* published in 1798. The short appoggiatura is played quickly. The long appoggiaturas must be notated in the same values they are to be given when played. Türk defines the principles of execution with greater precision than C. P. E. Bach and François Couperin.

The last section of commentary in the chapter on appoggiaturas deals with the unaccented appoggiatura *(Nachschlag)*, which was already in use at the beginning of the eighteenth century but had not been treated in any of the important German methods manuals. Despite the fact that they are written in the same type of notation (with small auxiliary notes) and can easily be confused in the execution of a musical passage, there is an essential distinction between the accented *(Vorschlag)* and unaccented *(Nachschlag)* appoggiaturas. The accented appoggiatura takes the value of the main note it precedes. The unaccented appoggiatura takes the value of the principal note it follows. Because the pages devoted to the discussion of this ornament are missing from Türk's book, an inference has been developed concerning the notation and execution of this particular ornament with reference to the contrasting embellishment, the short appoggiatura. Essential to this approach was Türk's own comparison of these two devices, which can be comprehended from the organization of his discussion of the ornaments.

Türk breaks the ornaments down into two basic groups depending on the mode of execution involved:

1) integral ornaments, the notation for which is included in the text (the interpretation therefore being based upon the actual written text); and

2) voluntary ornamentation, which is not contained in the text itself (the interpreter creating it in accordance with the written melody).

Familiarity has already been established with the most essential ornaments from the work of C. P. E. Bach (double appoggiatura [*Anschlag*], turn [*Doppelschlag*], slide [*Schleifer*], trill with suffix [*Triller mit Zusatz*], trill without suffix [*Triller ohne Zusatz*], descending trill [*Triller von oben*], ascending trill [*Triller von unten*], upper mordent [*Pralltriller*], mordent, acciaccatura [*Zusammenschlag*], combination ornaments, vibrato [*Bebung*] and the arpeggio).

The new upper mordent would be an exception here. Türk calls for an execution (b, c) which differs fundamentally from the examples in C. P. E. Bach's work (a).

The conventional marking is: (the first measure).

The last two examples (b, c) show that the short trill was gradually disappearing during this period. The first note of the short trill is executed from the principal note.

The turn marked above the note in Türk's passage differs in no way from Bach's example (a). What is new in Türk's observation (b) consists in the execution of the turn, which is marked over the note with a dot (see page 74).

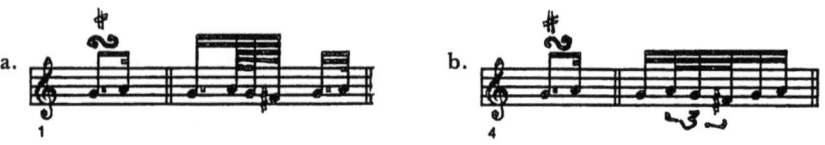

Türk's version is simpler and unquestionably easier from the point of view of the interpreter.

This chapter of Türk's *Klavierschule* is of importance from the practical point of view when it comes to interpretation of the ornaments in the musical literature of the eighteenth century, particularly the music of the classical period.

Turning now to Türk's methodology, he can be found in agreement on many points with C. P. E. Bach. He begins his program of instruction with an introduction to notation, mastery of the hand and the individual fingers and simple time exercises. The student then begins to work on simple pieces. Like C. P. E. Bach, Türk published 12 short pieces for beginners in an appendix. Türk's program of instruction proceeded along theoretical and practical tracks simultaneously: scales, keys (tonalities), intervals, chords, and exercises containing both simple and compound embellishments (to be played slowly and clearly) and calling for varying fingerings. The new here consists in the different dynamics. There would certainly be nothing new about a program of instruction which takes the student from pieces without accidentals to compositions with several sharps and flats, a method which accustoms him to this type of playing at the very beginning of his training. What is new in Türk's method, and in the methods generally, is the attention he gives to time and rhythm. The beginning of this training precedes technical finger proficiency. In the more advanced stages of development, the neglect of the rhythmical side of performance will have as a consequence an unsureness in matters of time, and this is a shortcoming which is very difficult to remedy. Türk brought new approaches to this aspect of keyboard training.

CHAPTER 5: PERFORMANCE

This chapter constitutes Türk's most important contribution to this problem in the eighteenth century. A number of ideas first found expression here regarding clarity in performance and punctuation, that is, phrasing and accented tones.

In the section of the chapter containing his general remarks, Türk offers his thinking on what constitutes good performance, on the importance of performance for practical musical application, the purpose of performance, and the feelings and emotions which contribute to poor performance.

Türk laid down the following principles as factors of good performance:

1) necessary proficiency in playing and reading the musical text, knowledge of the figured bass and comprehension of and an ability to analyze the composition;
2) clarity in execution;
3) proper understanding of the expression of the composition;
4) effective employment of ornaments and other devices;
5) a mature feeling for the emotion and passion the music conveys;
6) proper fingering; and
7) sureness of rhythm and time.

In the following sections of this chapter points 2, 3 and 4 will be looked at in some detail.

Türk was the first in the history of music theory to introduce the problem of clarity in execution, to study it in all its aspects and to define the elements comprising it. Clarity in execution will depend on the pure mechanical aspects; the emphasis given to certain tones (what are referred to as the accented tones); and proper linkage and separation between musical sections (phrasing).

Mechanical clarity means that even in the fastest passages and ornaments, each tone must be heard clearly, given its full time value and played at the proper dynamic level. Lack of clarity in playing will mean either that some notes have been omitted entirely or that they have not been played with maximum clarity and expression and have been attacked either too forcefully or too weakly. If a note is given less time than it is due, or held too long by keeping the key depressed unnecessarily, it will produce in the first instance a tone which does not satisfy and in the second a jumble of sound in which the tones blur or run together. Türk proceeds from the fundamental notion that the performer should execute a piece so as to make it comprehensible to the listener, for whom it therefore becomes important that, among other things, the individual tones be given their proper dynamic emphasis.

Türk elaborated his thinking as follows:
Which tones require emphasis (accentuation)?

1) tones which fall on the downbeat, or good, or strong, beat in a given measure

2) tones which following the cesura begin a new section, phrase or period
3) appoggiaturas
4) intervals which are dissonant with respect to the bass or which introduce a dissonant interval
5) syncopated notes
6) tones which do not belong to the diatonic context which are used for purposes of modulation
7) tones which in context are fairly long, high or deep
8) drop and lift tones (release tones)

A few remarks should be added concerning the first element on this list. In Türk's view, a good performer will emphasize not only main downbeat, but the secondary downbeat immediately following it as well. For the sake of clarity reference will be made to the downbeat as the primary accent and the second downbeat as the secondary accent. The secondary accent, which comes on the second downbeat, must be less pronounced dynamically than the primary accent. Simple time will have no more than two downbeats. In 4/4 time there are four beats, two strong and two weak.

The example below shows notes which must be played with roughly the dynamics indicated regardless of time value.

1.

The composer expressly marks the accent at certain points in the piece if the following renditions are not desired.

2.

Rule 1 above will govern if no dynamics are indicated or if no exception to it is required for any other reason.

Türk was most rigorous in his accentuation of the initial tones of the sections, phrases and musical thoughts of a composition. Today Türk's rule is interpreted such that "each initial tone of a period must be given distinctly greater emphasis than a regular downbeat" to mean that these initial tones are to be more or less accentuated depending on whether they begin a larger or smaller section of a whole; that is, an initial tone following a full harmonic cadence must be more heavily accented than an initial tone following a half-cadence or the smallest section.

The number of crosses in the example below indicates the degree of accentuation.

The most forcefully accented notes will be found in the first and ninth measures. These would be examples of accentuation of an initial note and then of an accent following a full harmonic cadence. In the third, fifth, seventh and tenth measures (i.e., the third beat in the tenth measure) the initial tones are less heavily accented than in the first case, these being the initial notes of Türk's "periods" (phrases and the smallest sections). The limiting consideration in this instance, however, is that only those initial tones will be accented more which come on a downbeat (first) part of measure. The a^1 in the sixth measure marked with a circle can therefore not be as heavily accented as the following h^1, despite the fact that, overall, this musical thought is to be played louder than the preceding thought. This situation will arise fairly frequently in the musical literature. In measures 2, 4, 6, 8 and 10 (initial tones only) the initial tones are given even less emphasis than in the preceding cases. Only the downbeats are involved here.

The table on the following page illustrates the appoggiaturas which are dissonant against the bass (a^1 and a^2), an interval which is dissonant against the bass (a^3), intervals which prepare dissonances (b), syncopated notes (c^1 and c^2), modulation tones (d^1 and d^2), marked highs in context (e^1) and marked lows (e^2).

Why are dissonant intervals and dissonant chords to be played with greater emphasis than consonant intervals and chords? C. P. E. Bach laid down the rule but offered no explanation. He was surely assuming that it would be obvious to anyone, emotion and passion, after all,

being expressed by dissonances. The sharper the dissonances, or the more dissonant the chord, in a text, the more dynamic the chord must be. In paragraph 32 on page 319, Türk offers two examples, which give a better idea of his thinking on this problem. The first example shows highly dissonant chords, which are played more loudly than the less dissonant chords in the second example.

Looking now at the last item on the list of elements requiring accentuation, Türk introduced the marking ⌢' for the release, referred to today as the "drop-lift," in his short sonatas for beginners.

Finally, Türk discusses another device which helps set off the passage, that is, an extension of the tone. Emphasis can be given to individual tones not only by means of a dynamic accent, but also by prolonging them slightly.

This device is employed only if the tones involved are of exceptional importance: if they have been altered or if they are the highest notes in that particular melody line. In most instances these will be tones carrying an accent. In Türk's view, it is not possible to identify each and every one of these situations, so it will inevitably be the interpreter who is going to have to analyze and feel them. As formulated by Türk, the rule means that a note can be extended by no more than half its value; the following note loses as much of its value as the preceding note gains in extension. This fine performance device is referred to today as the "agogic accent" and employed in the interpretation of music of virtually all periods. It was probably used even earlier, Couperin's "suspension," calling to mind this particular performance device. During the Romantic period it assumed a new form. The execution of this device was combined with a retardation in tempo and a delay in the beginning of the accentuated tone.

This concludes the discussion of tones requiring accentuation, that is, of the second aspect of point 2. Now look at a third aspect of point 2, namely, the linkage and separation of musical passages, what is referred to as musical punctuation.

Proper phrasing is very important in the performance of a composition. It requires thorough comprehension of musical thoughts and an ability to convey them clearly. As Türk himself declared, there had up to this point been no work in this area which treated the problem of musical punctuation. He devotes the second part of his sixth chapter to a thorough discussion of this important subject.

Türk's observations concerning the organization of musical thoughts establish a foundation for correct, logical performance.

Some are of the view that there is no need to use dots, dashes, rests and caesura. Punctuation was introduced into both music and language not to make a text easier to comprehend, but rather to prevent misunderstandings which could arise without punctuation. Anyone who knows musical punctuation comprehends the fact that a particular composition has not been written for him alone. Any commentary on this point must deal with three questions:

1) how to convey a musical thought coherently;
2) how to organize musical thoughts so as not to disrupt the beat pattern; and
3) how to identify the "resting places" in a long piece.

In his opening paragraph Türk begins with a comparison between musical performance and expression through the medium of the written word. It is by way of this comparison with punctuation used in written text that he attempts to shed light on errors in musical interpretation.

Incorrect punctuation in a written text can alter the meaning or create a meaning entirely different from the one intended. Illogical breaks in melodic passages will destroy the clarity of the presentation and result in a misstatement of the musical thoughts. They can even run counter to the musical sense of the piece itself. In linking notes together incorrectly and dividing musical thoughts where they should not be divided (the end of a musical phrase constituting the only exception here), "we are committing the same error a speaker would if he paused in the middle of a word and held his breath" (page 308, paragraph 19). These examples show a musical thought which has been divided incorrectly. Türk expresses this with the sixteenth rests.

Just as much of an error would be committed if in reading one came to the end of a phrase but continued on without stopping, even though the passage called for a pause at that point. The same thinking applies to the transmission of musical thoughts as well. With the conclusion of a musical thought a point is reached (Türk refers to it as a "resting place") beyond which comes the beginning of a new musical thought. When a player comes to a point of rest but at the same instant continues on, he is committing a major error.

In the first four measures of the example given here punctuation can be seen which runs counter to the musical sense of the passage: the execution would not take account of the pauses and tie the end of the phrase with the beginning of the next (rather than separating them from one another; see measures 6, 8, eighth rests).

Return now to the three questions above. First, how does one transmit musical thoughts coherently?

An unfinished musical thought should never be interrupted prematurely by removing a finger from a key or inserting a pause. Nor should a thought be interrupted in the bass line. Fingering plays an important role here. Incorrect fingering will disrupt the musical thought.

On the next page can be seen how the first example should be played:

OF THE 18TH CENTURY 81

In this example, measures 1 and 2 indicate incorrect fingering. The fingering in measures 3, 4, and 5 is more appropriate.

In measure 1, playing the G and the c following it with the same finger will create a short pause, which breaks up the thought in the bass.

Some will raise objections to Türk's subtle thinking concerning the factors contributing to coherent transmission of musical thought. The perceptive listener will hear the interruption in the bass because his concentration is not limited to developments in the top line. This subtlety is all the more critical considering the frequency with which it is offended against. Türk goes into this in some detail.

Now, how can musical thoughts be separated from one another without breaking up the beat structure in the process? The end of a melodic unit is signaled by removing the finger lightly from the last note played and then giving the first note of the following thought somewhat greater emphasis. To mark tones which should be accented more heavily Türk uses the sign ⋀ . This sign is still used for the accent today. Removing the finger lightly from the key establishes a short pause, separates the thoughts from one another and at the same time maintains the integrity of the beat structure.

In the last measure of the example below, Türk shows that the end of a phrase should in most instances be played more softly. The eighth rest in the last measure of example b separates the melodic phrase in the first two measures from the third and following measures.

If the composer himself indicates the pause following the last note of a melodic phrase (as in the last measure of the example here), Türk's thinking would not apply.

Finally, how does one identify the points of rest? In passages containing phrases and sections which may be difficult to identify, Türk introduces the punctuation mark " (to indicate a caesura). He uses it for the first time in his work on method and his short sonatas for beginning keyboard students to help the student begin to develop a solid understanding of phrasing from the very beginning of his instruction and to counteract arbitrariness in phrasing. In this connection Türk called for composers to show a more responsible attitude toward the problem of punctuation and to indicate it more clearly.

Türk's punctuation marks did not gain acceptance. He distinguishes points of rest which become obvious from the composer's notation. These are pauses.

The examples on the following page focus on the rests which are not indicated. This requires incomparably greater attention, thorough analysis of the horizontal line and, most importantly, good intuitive comprehension of the text, sensitive feeling, as Türk put it, because these are not separated from one another by pauses.

The individual examples here are set off from one another by the double bars. The points of separation are indicated by the punctuation mark ".

The search for the caesuras and the smallest units of melody are taken up from the very beginning of the composition, where it is established whether it begins with a complete measure or an incomplete measure. If it begins with an incomplete measure, it is then looked at more closely to see if this measure contains two or three or more eighth notes or notes of other values, because the caesuras will ordinarily fall on precisely the same part of the measure. This is illustrated in the second half of the example given previously in the first row, example number one, in the first row, number 2, in the third row, number 4 and in the second row, number three. But neither is this approach always reliable. Composers will try to add variety of the phrasing they employ. So in other pieces the rests will often be placed on other beats.

The method Türk puts forward for drilling students in problems of musical punctuation is suggestive. The instructor will have the student repeat the piece not from a note played incorrectly, but rather from the caesuras, the pauses and the rests. In this way the student begins to develop an ability to sense what goes together and what should be separated.

Türk concludes his discussion of punctuation with a reference to J. G. Sulzer's work entitled *Über die musikalische Interpunktion* (On Musical Punctuation) in his treatise *Allgemeine Theorie der schönen Künste* (General Theory of the Fine Arts), in the article *Performance (Vortrag)*, Leipzig, 1773.

The following is a brief summary of the key points concerning musical punctuation.

To convey a musical thought logically and coherently requires proper punctuation. Caesuras are every bit as important in music as they are in declamation; they must therefore be indicated in the written text. They are marked at the appropriate points in the music as written. Phrases cannot be interrupted with any release of the key if the sense of the music calls for a smooth transition from one part of the phrase to another. An integral musical thought cannot be broken up by contrived pauses. The close of a passage, be it a phrase, a period or a sentence, should in most instances be played decrescendo; the following note will then be given greater emphasis.

Today particular value is attached to Türk's pioneering efforts in this area of performance, which was in his time previously unresearched. His views found a successor in the following century (Hugo Riemann). Türk has still not lost his relevance in our time. We could not even conceive of the interpretation of works of the classical period, particularly the dance compositions and songs arranged for keyboard, without application of the understanding gained from this chapter.

AGOGICS

Türk treats the technique of departing from a basic tempo in detail. He discusses playing without set tempo; acceleration and retardation; and what is referred to as *tempo rubato*.

For the first time he indicates changes in tempo (accelerando and ritardando) with notational markings to prevent misunderstanding. Türk developed the following system of markings for the individual agogic elements:

1) Passages in which he wants a slow retard he marks as follows:

2) Individual musical thoughts which are not to be played at a gradually retarded tempo, but rather more slowly throughout, will be marked by the following sign:

3) Passages which are to be played at a gradually accelerated tempo have this marking:

Similar is the following marking:

Interestingly enough, Türk's markings found use by many composers and interpreters of his day. They would not find acceptance today, however.

With the exception of Couperin, earlier writers on keyboard method had expressed no views concerning the important interpretive devices that make up tempo rubato. The only explanation could be that they were altogether unfamiliar with them and so naturally would not even have been to write about them either. Couperin discusses only a couple of the elements of the tempo rubato (suspension and aspiration), but the form in which we know it today emerged only in the second half of the eighteenth century. The first mention of this rubato is found in Mozart's letters. Türk was the first to treat it theoretically and define it as a particular way to shorten, lengthen or, in effect, displace a note. In practical terms, to play in tempo rubato means to hold back something from the value of one note and give this difference to another note.

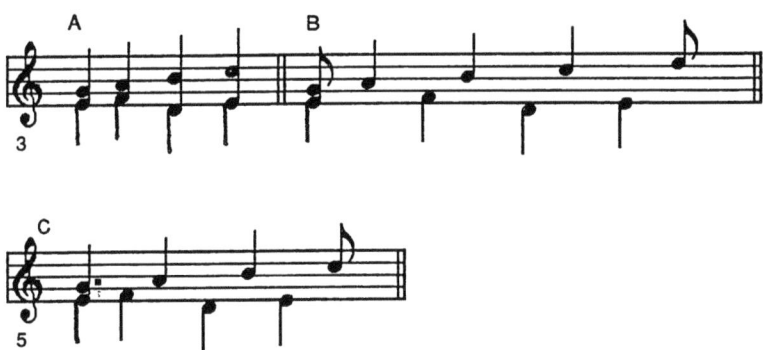

The first measure (example a) shows notes which are anticipated in measure 2 (example b). The upper, melodic, voice is thereby accelerated, while the lower voice continues at the original tempo. The time remains unchanged. In the third measure (example c) the notes are retarded. This type of agogic deviation, therefore, in effect displaces the notes in the melody at a particular point. German, accordingly, has two expressions for this device: "displaced" *(verücktes)* time and "stolen" *(verstohlenes)* time.

Practically speaking, of course, tempo rubato will not be found restricted to the confines of a single measure. Unlike what is seen in the case of Couperin, acceleration and retardation are in practice two aspects of an integral whole. Couperin linked suspension and aspiration in a single phrase. Herein lies the distinction between Couperin's ornament from the Baroque and Türk's agogic device of the classical period. In the former one sees only the first suggestion; in Türk one finds the whole.

The future will see Chopin emerge as the direct successor of Türk as a representative of these views.

SUMMARY

Türk's *Klavierschule* is a major work, not only in its comprehensiveness, but in its importance as well. It was in his day the most systematic of the keyboard methods—when it came to the practical aspects of keyboard performance and pedagogy, he omitted no detail. None of the earlier works on methods had treated problems in performance as exhaustively as Türk's. His greatest contribution lies in his discussions of musical punctuation, clarity in performance, and the agogic markings and their use. This imposing work marks the end of the period of the old musical instruments and of the forerunner of the fortepiano.

Chapter 4:
Johann Sebastian Bach and Wolfgang Amadeus Mozart

Johann Sebastian Bach

Johann Sebastian Bach left no written account of his work in the role of pedagogue. He did give instruction in keyboard instruments and in composition. Despite the fact that he had trained a number of noted artists who ultimately came to occupy prominent places in German musical culture, none of his former students left any personal account of Bach's instructional methods. One must therefore be contented with secondhand information. Little is known about how he conducted the lessons themselves. From the meager written sources available, one can only with difficulty develop the picture in any detail.

In the attempt to visualize Bach in his role as teacher, we can draw on the one memoir available, the book by Johannes Nikolaus Forkel, *Über das Leben, die Kunst and Kunstwerke von Johann Sebastian Bach* (The Life, Art and Artistic Works of Johann Sebastian Bach), published in Leipzig in 1802. The author of this book took no instruction from the master directly. He did have direct contact with his sons, Wilhelm Friedemann and Carl Philipp Emmanuel Bach. Most of the author's information has undoubtedly come from Bach's sons. For a study of Bach's keyboard methods, only two chapters are of importance: the second chapter, "Bach the Keyboard Player," and the seventh, "Bach the Teacher." The knowledge Forkel committed to the record included information concerning Bach's keyboard and organ playing. He offers a lively and detailed description of Bach as a performing artist, particularly of the technical side of his playing. He has less to say about Bach's playing from the artistic point of view. Interest here is confined to what concerns keyboard playing itself. Equally important for the subject will be Forkel's descriptions of Bach's instruction and his instructional methods as practiced during composition and keyboard lessons. Quotations appearing in the text have been taken only from Forkel's book (should no other source be given). The focus of attention will then shift to Bach's accomplishments in the area of keyboard technique. The most familiar section of the book deals with Bach's touch and fingering. For this reason attention will be concentrated primarily on these aspects of his method.

As can be visualized from the description, the hand position Bach employed at the keyboard differed from that of Couperin. With the hand held in Bach's position, "the 5 fingers will be arched such that the tips of the fingers form a straight line." Today the fingertips form an arch. The longest finger will be at the top of the arch, the shortest fingers, the first and the fifth, at the beginning and the end of the arch; that is, the fingers do not form a straight line. Held in Bach's position, the fingers correspond to the keys, fingers and keys parallel. Given this requirement, the parallelism between fingers and keys means that no finger can be brought nearer. "All fingers are held in equal readiness above the keys they are assigned to strike."

With the hand held in the position described above, the mechanics of applying the fingers to the keyboard from this position will be examined.

No finger must be allowed to drop onto a key or be driven down onto a key from its position above it. Rather "it must be manipulated by disciplined movement and with a feeling of the inner force." Each evidently wanted in fact to fix the position of the fingertips, an entirely unprecedented requirement for that time.

The force thus transmitted to the keys can be preserved not by raising the fingers back to a position directly above the keys, "but rather by allowing them to glide back over the front portion of the keys, gradually retracting the tips of the fingers back into the palms."

This type of touch is well known today and is used in the execution of rapid passages which are not to be rendered legato.

This gliding transition from one key to another quickly transmits the force and the pressure from one finger to the next "such that the tones are neither separated from one another nor overlap one another." They are neither too long nor too short, but precisely the length they are intended to be.

What results are achieved with a touch created in this way? The Bach touch offers a number of advantages at the hammerclavier, the clavichord and the organ.

First, the arched fingers facilitate all finger movements. Movements are not clumsy or hurried as would be seen in the case of players who play with extended or insufficiently arched fingers.

Second, by drawing the tips of the fingers back into the palms and transferring the force from one finger to another, one achieves maximum clarity with each note struck. This gives each individual passage a full, well-rounded sound, "as though each tone were a pearl." Through Forkel Bach had in fact turned a revolutionary phrase. The "pearly effect" would become the problem and essential characteristic of performance technique in the nineteenth century.

The touch Bach prescribed gives purpose and economy to motion as well, enabling the hand to economize in the application of its strength. Short, smooth finger motion places much less of a burden on the hand than sweeping, extended movements (as can be seen in the case of players who raise their fingers high above the keys).

> Bach moved only the last joints in his fingers. The hand kept its rounded shape over even the most thankless of passages. The fingers were raised only slightly above the keys, and they would remain in this position for the execution of trills as well. When one finger was busy, the others remained motionless.

It can be seen that Bach preferred purposeful movements and avoided anything which might tire the fingers or hand. He looked at motion over the shortest distance. "Other parts of the body would contribute even less to his playing." This sentence today really is history. The musical literature of the time required the player not to move any other parts of the body whatsoever. Thanks to Forkel's description of Bach's playing and the touch he employed, the motions Bach made when he played can be very easily visualized. It helps formulate the question of posture at the instrument, given the fact that this is very closely related to the elements previously referred to.

Forkel has not left a description of Bach's posture at the instrument, but for the palms to remain rounded and the fingers to keep their arch, which made it possible to hold them in a straight line, Bach could sit neither too high nor too low. He most likely played with a relaxed locomotor apparatus, because it is known that Bach insisted on an efficient, purposeful motion which would not tire the muscles and the hand.

As has already been mentioned, his son, C. P. E. Bach, emphasized the need to play with well-rested hands, and one can assume that he took this thinking from his father.

Since Forkel's account makes it clear that Bach attached great importance to the development of a well-rounded keyboard technique, an examination will now be made of some other aspects of that technique, beginning with the action of the fingers.

Because of the difference in the size and strength of the fingers, pianists will frequently tend to rely on the stronger fingers and disregard the weaker ones. A product of this tendency is a lack of uniformity in touch and a certain inadequacy which will make it difficult for a performer to execute clearly any passages in a piece for which he cannot establish his own fingering. J. S. Bach, of course, was fully aware of this shortcoming. In an attempt to remedy the situation he wrote special pieces which required the student to use all fingers of both hands in all possible positions and combinations to be able to play the pieces with the desired clarity.

Bach himself played compositions (études) which he was able to play because of his well-rounded finger technique:

> All fingers were equally strong and capable, so that it was with the greatest of ease that he could play parallel intervals, all types of runs and both single and double trills with both hands simultaneously.

When it came to different combinations of two voices in one hand, trills combined with the melody line, for example, he could dispose of these without difficulty as well.

Articulation, which today is regarded as an aspect of artistic performance, was in Bach's day another aspect of the technical side of keyboard performance. The way Bach played differed substantially from the way his contemporaries and predecessors played. Forkel explains the situation in the following terms:

> Bach would choose ten equally capable interpreters and have them play the same piece. In the end, each player would have played the piece differently, each playing with a different tone and achieving a different degree of clarity.

Assuming that all students had followed the same course of development and had achieved the same level of proficiency, the only explanation for the difference in the impression they left would lie in the touch each employed. The more proficient the artist, the greater the clarity of his playing. Confronted with a performance in which the player achieves only a minimal degree of tonal clarity, the listener is forced to focus his attention to the point where it becomes extremely difficult to follow the flow of the music. Listening to a performance in which the execution is of a higher degree of tonal clarity, the audience need not strain for the details; it can concentrate attention on the musical ideas and the relationships between them. This is an indication that the interpreter has to a great degree perfected his touch. And it was precisely this clarity and sharpness in each individual tone which set Bach apart as a performer. Forkel saw this to constitute the essential distinction between Bach and his contemporaries. Expressing it in today's terms, one would say that Bach had mastered his articulation to perfection.

As has been seen, when it came to this problem of articulation, C. P. E. Bach expressed a somewhat different point of view in his work. He adopted a compromise solution, although he offered no explanation as to how the student might achieve the desired aim:

> ...the playing of many has a gummy sound, as though the player has glue between his fingers. In attempting to compensate, some will play everything so quickly, the listener would think the keys were hot. This, however, creates an equally bad impression. The best solution would be to take a middle course.

One might legitimately question whether for the art of interpretation today it would come as something new and original to hear that the pianist must give attention to the clarity of his articulation, particularly when it comes to compositions of the pre-Romantic period. This surely does not constitute any new discovery, but one has only to recall how many different rules have been heard which purport to govern the stylistic interpretation of Bach's compositions and how contradictory they all are. Teachers do continuous battle with the problems involved here and search unceasingly for fundamental, immutable rules, which could stand against any objection. Forkel's work contains a number of observations which might qualify here, commentary which without question reflects an authentic Bach tradition. They were passed on to him directly by sons and students of Johann Sebastian Bach, whose statements we can probably take at face value. A clear, precise articulation is thus one of the conditions essential to proper interpretation of the works of J. S. Bach.

What follows now is a brief summary of what we have learned about Bach's playing and the characteristic features of his keyboard art:

1) each note played with expression
2) beautiful touch (cantabile tone)
3) all fingers trained to uniform capability
4) smooth, efficient finger movement
5) sharp, clear playing

Proceeding on the basis of these preconditions Bach himself developed a high degree of finger proficiency and mastery of the instrument.

The discussion so far has dealt exclusively with the advantages of Bach's technique. And there can be no doubt that the technical perfection of his playing alone would have been sufficient to establish him as the supreme, incomparable interpreter of keyboard music in the musical world of his day. But the artistic side of his playing is surely also worthy of examination.

Very little is known today about the artistic, interpretational aspects of Bach's playing. They were perhaps not described because at this time there was no conceptual apparatus adequate to the task available and the essential principles governing artistic performance were not yet fully understood. Instruction, too, was based upon examples (see Bach's remark in Chapter 7 of Forkel's account: "This is the way it should sound"; as to why, Bach did not say). As far as Bach's performance from the artistic point of view is concerned, nothing is known today of instructions governing methodology. It is known that Bach himself was an outstanding interpreter, and not only from the technical point of view. His entire artistic personality, of course, is proof enough of his profound musical sense. In the two statements below, Forkel, our most important source, confirms this as well:

> In playing his own compositions Bach would ordinarily establish a lively tempo and then play them each time with such interesting variation the music would speak to the listener as the living word.
>
> Bach generated force and passion not with any powerful physical attack on the keyboard, but rather by drawing on inner resources, harmony and melodic expression.

At least some idea of tempo is known, that is, Bach's fast-paced tempo, the reference here evidently being to his allegro works. It is also known how he created the dynamics at the dynamic climaxes of his pieces. His tempo must also have incorporated certain agogic nuances for his playing to have spoken to audiences as "the living word." He held their attention by his phrasing of the musical thoughts. It was precisely because he created his dynamics in response to inner forces that he did not indicate them in his pieces. He did make exceptions, however.

Also, no pedal markings will be found (the clavichord had no pedal; neither did the harpsichord in the sense of the pedals of the piano known today).

Phrasing and articulation are linked by rhythm. Bach must also have been without error when it came to rhythm.

Bach's favorite instrument was the clavichord. This instrument offered a number of advantages, which was why Bach thought so highly of it. The clavichord could produce shadings, nuances, of tones; it could augment or diminish a tone by a fourth; it was to some extent capable of variations in volume; and it could produce a vibrato sound *(Bebung)*. The instrument was capable of expressing "the most delicate thoughts." It can be seen from Forkel's account that Bach preferred the clavichord, because it was on this instrument that he could express his innermost emotions. He held the harpsichord in lower esteem; to him it seemed soulless. "The hammerclavier was just in its infancy in Bach's time, so neither could it offer him any satisfaction." If one knew nothing of Bach's creative activity, knew nothing of Bach the man and had available only the account left by Forkel, one would still see him as a musician distinguished by power of expression, profundity and emotion.

Returning to questions of technique, when it comes to fingering, Bach stands as a figure of truly revolutionary importance in the development of keyboard methods. He turned entirely away from the fingering which had established itself in the fourteenth century and survived into the second half of the eighteenth.

During Bach's youth, the clavichord available to composers was a fretted instrument; that is, several keys would strike a single string. It could not be pure-tempered, for which reason composers tended to avoid keys based on the black keys. Only those keys were used in which it was possible to achieve the purest tuning. This created a situation in which even the greatest of contemporary players played without using the thumbs, unless, of course, they were required for the extended intervals and octaves. Bach turned away from the familiar church modes and combined the diatonic and chromatic systems. In his later years he enjoyed the use of a well-tempered klavier and an unfretted clavichord and so began to use all keys. Forkel writes that Bach could tune his own instruments and "tempered his instrument so as to enable him to play on it in all 24 keys." Under these circumstances, he must unavoidably have come up against the inadequacy of the traditional fingering, which led him to develop a new fingering system, with which he could play in all 24 keys. "What had hitherto been the least used of the fingers, the thumb, had now become the most important." The new priority now assigned the thumb, together with its new occupation, were defined by new tasks. Couperin, whose fingering system was very different from the Bach fingering, was another composer who made frequent use of the thumb. Bach, however, made the thumb the focus of attention, the principal finger, because in the more difficult keys it was simply not possible to get along without it. Couperin had neither written nor played in the difficult keys; he had no real reason to. If a comparison is made between Couperin's fingering and Bach's, it can be seen that with the latter one can play anything smoothly and cleanly, whereas with Couperin's system one can at most get through his own compositions, but even then, only with a certain amount of difficulty.

Turning now to Bach's instructional method, the only basis upon which to develop any conception thereof is the seventh chapter of Forkel's account entitled "Bach the teacher." It must be admitted, however, that the map of the Bach method remains mostly blank. From the accounts which have come down to us we know only something about his touch and can glean a crumb or two of information concerning the way he conducted his composition lessons. Forkel also tells us something about the kind of musical literature Bach used for instructional purposes.

Look once again for a moment at Bach's touch. It is certainly no coincidence that in Forkel's account of Bach's work as a teacher, the problem of touch stands as the first and most important problem for all beginners. Forkel suggests that Bach without doubt gave special attention to the development of a particular type of touch with the objective of achieving a certain quality of sound. A course of instruction with Bach would therefore begin with drills to develop a touch characteristic of Bach alone. "To accomplish this, his beginning students would over a course of many months play only individual musical sentences." These were most certainly études which Bach would compose on the spot during a lesson. These "études" took the form, among other things, of short preludes and two-part inventions. "Musical sentences were played with both hands and all fingers as drills in which the student strove to produce tones which rang clear and pure." Teachers today know very well how much patience an average student must summon to develop a proper cantabile touch, and this patience is required not only on the part of the student, but also on the part of the teacher. Bach himself was so patient that "for a bored student he would write short pieces, into which he appropriately wove his sentence drills." Bach comprehended the nature of touch as an aspect of technique and for this reason added to the title page of his two-part inventions that these pieces had been composed for the purpose of "developing a cantabile style of playing." Later, once the student had developed his mastery of touch, he would move on to longer and more challenging compositions, which, once again, Bach himself provided.

Bach would try to ease the burden on his students by playing the compositions he wrote for them all the way through for them, then declaring: "That's the way it should sound." A teacher, for whom the beauty of the tone is one of the most precious of qualities, cannot escape the responsibility he has to demonstrate this quality himself during the instruction of his students. If he cannot himself sit at the keyboard and play, he will not be in a position to tell his students how the piece should sound either. Every teacher should take Bach's method as an example; if he cannot demonstrate the proper execution of an entire piece he wants a student to study, he should give particular attention to at least certain passages in the piece (and, of course, demonstrate how these should be played) and the quality of tone the composition calls for, for this cannot be conveyed by the spoken word.

Compared with Couperin's approach, as well as that of his own son, Bach's progressive method was a rigorous, acid test for all his beginners. C. P. E. Bach writes in his *Versuch* that as soon as they had mastered touch, his father's students would have to begin immediately to accustom themselves to his demanding compositions. The best evidence in favor of Bach's method was the musical education of his own sons, who were all outstanding musicians and pianists.

In Bach's time there were no virtuosos whose training had concentrated on one instrument only. Each musician was required to develop a thorough mastery of the principles of figured bass and the composer's craft. He had to be able to play several instruments, conduct and, if necessary, step in as accompanist as well. By force of these circumstances, instruction proceeded in a number of directions simultaneously.

Bach did not begin his instruction in composition in the traditional way with dry counterpoint theory. Nor did he take the time to go into the details of tone relations; this he left to the theoreticians and instrument makers.

> He started his students from the very beginning with problems in four-voice figured bass. They would then later be assigned to write their own chorales. In all his assignments he required not only purity in the harmony, but that the tones in each voice be linked together naturally to establish a solid, continuous line.

> The individual voices were to him as those of living persons speaking to one another within a closed circle. If there are three, one can remain silent from time to time and listen to the others until he can think of something else to say himself.

On the basis of Forkel's brief description of Bach's approach to instruction in composition, one might leap hastily to the conclusion that the greatest of polyphonists had no appreciation for counterpoint theory. It would appear, rather, that Bach was simply rejecting dry formulas and lifeless schemes and stereotypes which had become axiomatic for some of his contemporaries. The important thing for Bach, clearly, was that the music live. He would allow his students freedom to transgress some of the rules of composition if in so doing they were not detracting from the sound of the whole or contradicting the inner sense of the piece. Bach clearly confirms today's view that he allowed his students great freedom of expression and did not attempt to break down the personality of students who happened to display a degree of individuality. This can serve as an example of Bach's artistic sense, rather than of any particularly deep respect for methodological doctrines.

Forkel's other comments tell something about the musical literature Bach chose for his students. "Beyond the compositions of the master, Bach's students played nothing but classical works for the duration of his course of instruction." Detailed study of true musical works of art developed in them an instinct for beauty. "The best education consists in accustoming young people to what is good." Good musical taste could then never be driven out entirely, even if forced by adverse circumstances under the influence of inferior music. The education of the young based upon the best examples in the musical literature and the instinct for beauty this cultivates needs no further comment.

SUMMARY

J. S. Bach's contribution consists in the following:

1) He probably devoted his knowledge and understanding to the clavichord.
2) In the view of J. S. Bach's son, C. P. E. Bach, his father's instructional methodology consisted essentially in having his students play challenging pieces of his own composition from the very beginning of the course of instruction.
3) On posture at the instrument there is no information.
4) Bach introduced the arched hand configuration employed today.
5) He was first to require fixed finger positions.
6) Like Couperin, Bach attached importance to the beauty of the tone.

7) Bach anticipated what today is referred to as hand mechanics (*Motorik*).

Wolfgang Amadeus Mozart

Mozart's playing inspired rapturous universal admiration. It is also known that he gave keyboard instruction and that the number of his students remained very small. To uncover new information concerning Mozart, the teacher, and his interpretational art is no small task. Countless studies have been published on the creative aspects of Mozart's career. Every music history contains an account in which one can read about young Wolfgang Amadeus, the wonder child, whose playing would send listeners into raptures. There are, however, no factual descriptions of his playing itself, neither from his childhood nor from his later years. Of his teaching methods we likewise know only very little.

Even J. N. Hummel, who studied with Mozart and most certainly held his teacher in the highest esteem, left no memoir of the period of his study with the master. There is only one source of information available to us—Mozart's own letters, most importantly his letters to his father. There are extracted passages from three letters which can help develop a fairly clear picture of just what it was that Mozart valued and what he criticized as negative in the interpretational aspect of performance. (Extracts from Wolfgang Amadeus Mozart, *Briefe* [Letters], Berlin, 1964.)

In a letter to his father dated October 24, 1777, Mozart describes the playing of the daughter of the noted piano builder Stein:

> Whoever sees and hears his daughter play and can still keep from laughing has to be made of stone like her father. Instead of sitting in the middle of the keyboard, she sits all the way up in front of the treble, where she has more chances to move around and make grimaces. She rolls her eyes around and smirks. When she repeats a passage, she plays it more slowly the second time through. If she plays it a third time, she takes it even more slowly. . . . When she plays a passage, she has to raise her arms as high as possible. Whatever the markings for a passage indicate, it is the arm, not the fingers, which must provide the effect, and this in a painstakingly heavy, clumsy manner. The most hilarious thing, though, is that when she comes to a passage which should flow like oil, but during which she is required to substitute fingers, she does not give it the least thought; rather, when the time comes, she simply leaves out the notes, raises her hand and picks up again as comfortably as you please—by which technique you might more reasonably expect to hit a wrong note and one which frequently produces a curious effect. I am writing this for no other reason than to give Papa some conception

of clavichord playing and instruction he can draw some benefit from later. Herr Stein is absolutely crazy about his daughter. She is 8 and a half years old and learns everything by heart. She can succeed. She does have a great deal of talent, but she will not go anywhere this way. She will never be able to play very fast, for she seems bound and determined to do everything she can to make her hands heavy. She will never develop the most essential and the most difficult and the most important requisite in music, namely, time, because she has done everything possible from her earliest years not to play in time. Herr Stein and I discussed this point for a good two hours at least ... but I think I've almost brought him around now, because he asks me what I think about almost everything. He used to be absolutely crazy about Beecke, but now he can see and hear that I can play better than Beecke, that I do not grimace all the time, and yet at the same time I can play with such expression that, as he himself confesses, I have been able to get better results from his fortepianoes than anyone else so far. Everyone is amazed that I can keep accurate time. What they cannot comprehend is that in tempi rubato in an adagio, the left hand is supposed to remain independent, as though it knew nothing about what the right is doing. In their case the left hand will follow along.[1]

In the letter of January 17, 1778, he describes Vogler's playing, Vogler having played the Lützow concert together with Mozart:

> He played the first piece prestissimo, the Andante allegro and the Rondo really prestissimo. The bass he played for the most part differently from the way it was written, and every now and then he would even make up an entirely new harmony and melody.
>
> You really cannot do anything else at that speed. Your eyes cannot see it, and the hands cannot play it. So, what good is it then? This kind of sight-reading and [word omitted? — TR] both come down to one and the same thing as far as I am concerned. Listeners [and here I mean only those who really deserve the name] will only be able to say they have seen music and somebody playing the clavichord. They listen to him, think and actually experience as little as he in the process. You can easily imagine how insufferable it all was, because I simply could not bring myself to say to him, Much too fast! Besides, it is much easier to play something fast than it is to play it slowly. After all, you can always leave out a few notes in certain passages without anybody even noticing. But is this really what you would call beautiful? ...[2]

And in a letter of September 26, 1781, Mozart writes as follows:

> ...for just a man in such a towering rage can be expected to overstep the bounds of order and moderation and lose control of himself entirely, so, too, must the music forget itself. On the other hand, no matter how violent the passions, they should never be expressed to revolting excess. Even in the most horrifying situations, the music must never displease

the ear. To the contrary, it must always give the ear pleasure; that is, it must always remain music. This is why I did not choose a key unrelated to f [the key of the aria], but rather one congenially related to f. Not the next one, D minor, but rather the one beyond that, A minor.[3]

Based on the views expressed in these passages, the following conclusions can be drawn:

1) Mozart rejected everything artificial and any form of mimicry intended to express experience through the performer's playing. He would surely have rejected all affectation in playing as well. This does not mean, however, that the playing would have lost any of its power of expression. So Mozart required that playing be natural and simple.

2) In the case of Stein's daughter, Mozart criticized her cumbersome style at the keyboard, her "heavy" hands. Cumbersome playing and the heavy hand are the result of incorrect hand position. When a player raises his arms and hands too high he encumbers the elbows and wrists and, ultimately, interferes with the development of proper finger technique. It can now be seen that Mozart attached importance to natural hand position, lightness in playing and relaxed hands. He also criticized the Stein girl's posture and positioning at the keyboard.

3) Mozart held that the most important thing in music is tempo. He was not referring to speed, but rather to proper, proportionate tempo, and particularly to evenness in rhythm. "Everyone is amazed that I can keep accurate time." This means that, ordinarily, no particular importance was attached to this prerequisite of good playing, as Mozart and later Türk were to do. Compositions from the classical period, and particularly those of Mozart, cannot be properly executed without giving this aspect of performance its due.

4) Mozart expressed himself in no uncertain terms in criticizing the tendency to play too fast. This practice altered the character of the composition and detracted from the expressiveness of the playing. It leads to technical inaccuracy (omissions of notes, lack of clarity in execution, etc.) as well. Virtuosity for the sake of virtuosity was not among the devices Mozart employed in his playing. On this point he is in agreement with the thinking of C. P. E. Bach. (See page 174 of appendix.)

5. Frédéric Chopin and Franz Liszt

Frédéric Chopin

After several short voyages to Berlin, Dresden, and Prague to see the famous virtuosos of that time, Chopin gave his first concert in Vienna in 1829. As the music critic who was the correspondent of Leipzig's *Allgemeine Musikalische Zeitung* said in the November 18th, 1829, edition, Chopin became "a meteor in the sky of the music world,"[1] excelling in his tender touch and masterful dexterity. Particularly, his carefully nuanced interpretation, full of feeling and melacholic features, has been described as genius. As a contemporary of Franz Liszt, Chopin lived almost forty years less, so that we have an even less full picture of Chopin's pedagogical activity than that of Liszt.

Chopin knew all of the prominent people in Paris of his time and had lived a full social life in the salons of the Parisian aristocracy. He had been known not only as a piano virtuoso and composer, but also as a pedagogue. He regularly gave lessons and probably enjoyed teaching. Chopin had only one student whom he classified as a genius, a boy, Filtsch, from Hungary. Liszt described this boy's talent as follows: "When that small one begins to play, I will close my shed."[2] Filtsch died at the age of fifteen in 1845. Most honored among Chopin's students were the Polish students Marcelina Czartoryska and Karol Mikuli. Chopin's students were not so talented as Liszt's, but he prepared many outstanding pianists: L. Sloper, B. Richards, K. Hartman, Adolf Gutmann, K. Lysberg, Georges-Amédée-Saint-Clair Mathias, Camille O'Meara (née Camille Dubois), Vera Rubio (née Kologrivoff), Countess Elise Peruzzi (née Eustafiew), Thomas Dyke Acland Tellefsen, K. Wernik, G. Schumann, W. Steinbrecher, and Polish students Delfina Potocka, Fryderika Streicher (née Müller), and Zofia Zaleska (née Rosengardt).

Opinions about American pianist Louis Moreau Gottschalk (1829–

1869) vary. Some allege that he was Chopin's student for a short period, but others assert that "only [what] was sure, ... he played before Chopin."[3]

For the considerations on Chopin's silhouette as a pedagogue, there are only a few materials available from accessible sources. Marcelina Czartoryska, Karol Mikuli (who was director of the Conservatory of Music in Lvov), Camille Dubois (later, when married, O'Meara), G. Mathias (professor at the National Conservatory of Music in Warsaw), Fryderika Streicher, and Zaleska were the students and later friends of Chopin who preserved the statements of the master in interviews, articles, and in introductions to the editions of Chopin's music. The first research on Chopin was begun twenty years after his death, by Jan Kleczyński, who in 1869 published the first article in Warsaw, in the periodical "Bluszcz." Kleczyński later continued by arranging three conferences on Chopin in Warsaw. The proceedings were published in 1880, in Paris. The posthumous essay of Professor Tarnowski, historian of literature, appeared in 1895. Alexander Michalowski, a well-known Polish pianist, published an interview with Karol Mikuli in 1932, in the edition of M. Gliński. Huneker's book on Chopin was published in 1922. These sources will form the starting point of the deliberations on Chopin's method of teaching the piano, and on his interpretation of music. It is known that Chopin left behind fragmentary notes on methodical issues. The notes of his future methods unfortunately remained at a preliminary stage. Chopin never finished this projected major work. After his death, Chopin's sister gave the manuscript to Princess Marcelina Czartoryska. Jan Kleczyński published the notes of Chopin in German in the edition *Chopins grössere Werke* (Chopin's Major Works), with a short preface (pages 3-5), "Notizzen zur Méthode des Méthodes," in Leipzig (1898) by Breitkopf & Härtel.

In this profile of Chopin all of the materials mentioned above will be used, as well as others, in faithfully trying to reconstruct Chopin's method of the piano and the style of his lessons, as well as pianistic ideals on the interpretation of music, especially his own.

The former students of Chopin who were interviewed are mostly older, so their statements may be veiled by sentiments and time, and by the selective quality of their memories. However, these materials do not differ on the theme of Chopin's technique and on interpretive issues, such as phrasing and the so-called tempo rubato.

Without exception all of the former students interviewed agree on one point: that Chopin was reserved in discussion. He was exact and thorough in his teaching, but nonetheless enthusiastic during lessons.

"His students adored him."⁴ Karol Mikuli, the most talented student of the master, once complained: "My *forté* had stunned Chopin and not once from this reason I suffered."⁵ Mikuli had a harsh and dry forté, and Chopin already in his first lessons warned him from making a stronger attack, because it is difficult to remove a harsh attack in a short time.

ANALYSIS OF CHOPIN'S PERFORMANCE

The first characteristic which distinguishes Chopin from other artists who were celebrated in London, Vienna, Leipzig, and Berlin is his touch (from French *touché*; i.e., the attack on a key by a finger). In general, his attack was "more gentle" than was ordinarily adopted.⁶ He rarely used much forté, since it produced a harsh and artificial sound. In Mikuli's references Chopin was irritated by hardness in the strike. We are told that he avoided a too strong and "glittering accent."⁷ Does this mean that he did not like frequent accentuation? How can this statement be reconciled with the accents in his mazurkas and ballades? Should one accentuate Chopin's music rarely? Assuredly, Chopin's markings signify real accents in his mazurkas. Would frequent accentuation take away the poetry of his long phrases, as in his Scherzo in B-flat Minor, the second theme with the flowing accompaniment in the left hand?

Did Chopin avoid regular accents, that is, the specific category of accents which underline the metric beat in a piece? Chopin's harmony, its flow, the type of musical phrases or ideas, periods, motives, and the whole melody, after serious study, will tell us how destructive zealously played metric accents would be. In this case, Michalowski is not able to give notions consistent with the truth.

Chopin preferred to play with a pretty, "delicate attack"; and therefore, if some student played "rolling the piano," with excessive force, Chopin asked him, "What's that? A dog barking?"⁸ This famous sentence indicates another feature of his deliberations: From the beginning Chopin laid the foundations of the freedom or relaxation of the hands during play, trying to remove spasmodic or convulsive movements of the hand, and consequently, of the fingers, along with all possible stiffness of the playing apparatus. Only a sensitive, not a coarse, attack of the fingers and an unconvulsive, free hand could produce cultured, agreeable play. That is why Chopin disagreed with forced harsh playing and called it "the barking of a dog." This does not mean that Chopin did not have a powerful tone, and that one should avoid any stronger gradations and accents in the interpretation of Chopin today.

When it was necessary in the interpretation, for instance of Beethoven or Mendelssohn, as Mikuli notes, Chopin instinctively had a deep and strong attack, even enough to reach a round *forté* on today's pianos.

The most convincing argument of Mikuli—"When Chopin wrote forté, he understood forté"—reaches deeper into the substance of Chopin's music. Chopin's music possesses a wide spectrum of feelings, from the titanic to the most intimate, sometimes going beyond the frame of technical possibilities of instruments of his time. Mikuli further furnishes proof that Chopin *in cantabile* could reach a powerful tone.[9]

The French pianos of the first half of the nineteenth century need to be taken into account. At this point, the construction of the instrument was at the beginning stages of its evolution into the present. The French pianos were small and slim, and were noted for their facile action and delicate sound. Forté, as we conceive it, sounded very harsh. The present-day pianos, Steinways, Baldwins, Blütners, Bösendorfers, and Petrofs, have a round and sonorous forté tone. Chopin's tone, nevertheless, was not an orchestral tone in today's understanding of the term. Chopin liked to play Erards pianos, but preferred to compose on the Pleyels, because of their more darkened, obscured sound.

On the Pleyel, Chopin composed the Préludes, the Scherzo in B-flat Minor, and the Fantasy in F Minor. No wonder that his first considerations were dedicated to the production of a refined attack, and therefore, of a "beautiful" tone. Chopin required the same perfection from his students, even in their first lessons, becoming a real torturer. The base of his method relied on the refinement of the attack. Also the playing of Liszt himself did not always satisfy Chopin. Both Beethoven and Liszt played incredibly skillfully, but with a less refined touch.

Whence does this preoccupation with a beautiful tone and a sensibility for delicacy emanate? Chopin's education favored the writers with high artistic taste, delicacy, and the purest forms. Not Beethoven, but rather Mozart, was Chopin's preferred composer. Lying on his deathbed, Chopin begged Marcelina Czartoryska and the violoncellist Franchôme to play the sonatas of Mozart. Even in Mozart's *Don Juan,* his favored *chef-d'oeuvre,* some passages had been "unpleasant to his ear"[10]: Chopin had a high and profound conception of ideal piano playing.

In order to complete the deliberations on Chopin's "pretty and harmonious" playing, there are no other reliable references except those of Kleczyński's and Michalowski's articles and Huneker's short notes, all acquired from the contemporaries of Chopin. Huneker's short analysis does not contain any word on the theme of Chopinistic rubato;

but, nevertheless, it remains the most comprehensive, although it is a compilation.

As Frédéric Chopin played, so he composed, in his unique and individual manner. His contemporaries agreed without exception that he played with enthusiasm. "His scales had been pearly," as Huneker mentions, "the attack was full, sweet, elastic, and *cantabile*. His technique did not know any difficulties."[11] That is why each of his fingers was a subtly different voice with the unusual faculty for the creation of a tone. "Chopin often played the same composition in a different manner, changing the tempo, the *timbre* of the sound, and even in the nuances."[12] He was able to inspire his instrument so much that "the tone took on a somewhat unearthly coloration, having nothing in common with the prime nature of the tone. The beautiful tone of his play, the transparent harmony, fluent tone, and the pedalling presented the public with an almost supernatural joy."[13] The brightness, smoothness, and lightness of Chopin's playing are connected with his fantastic temperament, his poetical melancholy, his innovations in his artistic ideals, and also his physical temperament.

CHOPIN'S METHOD

As the first condition of Chopin's method, one should consider the refined attack *(touché)*. Chopin's theories on this and other important subjects were explicated in his "Projet de Méthode" (Sketch for a Method). Chopin knew that a sensible and precise attack required training in the very first lesson, regarding the correct positioning of the hand. This position was that of a slightly rounded hand, as accepted by the German methods. To Chopin his hand position was advantageous and also gracious. It was prepared by casting the hand lightly on the keyboard so that the fingers were not arched, but stretched a little, and leaned against the keys E, F-sharp, G-sharp, A-sharp, B and so on, the position of the E major scale, which was the easiest position in Chopin's method.

Without changing this position, training began with exercises, assuring the independence of the fingers; the first, in *staccato* articulation, was complemented by the relaxation of the wrist. The hand was held as if suspended in air, feeling no weight. While "throwing the hand downwards, the player did not feel any weight."[14] The fingers did not attack the keys in an entirely curved, inwardly bent, or even rounded position, but with the soft part placed under the edge of the finger. This attack required a consequently less rounded hand, sometimes giving the impression that Chopin's and his students' hands lay totally flat on the keyboard, an impression which will be explained later. This position even implies the negative idea that it is difficult to understand how Chopin could play with such a hand position.

The second main principle of Chopin's method assures equal force in all the fingers, eliminating inferiority of the fourth and fifth fingers. This is achieved through the type of exercise shown in the example below. In addition, the third condition of Chopin's method, the "weightless" relaxation of the wrist, is a totally modern idea. (All of the examples are from Kleczyński, *op. cit.*, page 38.)

The next series of exercises consisted of the staccato-legato (today's term for portando articulation) or heavy staccato, in which the finger stayed longer on the key. This is understood to be stopped, concentrated on the attack.

Then, at last, the real legato, "jeu lié," modifying the staccato-legato play into the accentuated legato, by using the fingers and the wrist. From the beginning all of these exercises had to be executed pianissimo; in order, it must be supposed that the attack not be harsh or stiff or fatigued. In addition, a slow, quiet approach makes the player aware of the loosening of the wrist and hand.

This same exercise then should be played later as sounding fully legato, but executed as the attack by bent fingers, lifted up—"Ein und Aufwärtsbiegen"[15]—and finally executed by precise legato, with the fingers more or less accentuating with metronomic evenness, modifying the dynamic scale of ff-pp, and in movements slow at the beginning, later gradually moving from andante to prestissimo.

After the formation of the fine attack and the fine tone has thoroughly taken over all sorts of articulation, including the relaxation concept, comes the next step in Chopin's method: The scales and the exercise series which preserve the "tranquil form"[16] of the hand. It was necessary to know how to lead the hand by a fluid and facile movement to the right or the left, depending on whether the scale ascended or descended, the same in a passage, with the thumb turned down or in the opposite direction, if the longer fingers (third or fourth) crossed above the thumb. Chopin presented this movement by non-sounded glissandi on the keyboard, a good pictorial manner. Kleczyński further offers many sentences on this problem: In the moment of laying the thumb under or of crossing the thumb over, in scales, "usually at the beginning the students could not avoid moving the elbow or twisting the hand a little.... Chopin insisted on holding the hand in the same position."[17] For that reason he even "preferred for the first time a less legato play."[18]

He tried to say that the even sound of the executed scales presumed not only strong and well-trained fingers, but mainly the initial hand position in which the elbow stays near the body and the turning down of the thumb is unnoticed, as one may observe in the great pianists.

Why has so much space been donated to the process of the composition of the attack? Of the Chopinistic touch? If the fundamental basis of Chopin's method, the perfecting of the attack, is looked at, one must grant him unusual value. The schools in his century completely forgot this message. The outstanding education of the whole mechanism of technique absorbed much of the energy of many good pianists, gradually eroding the sensibility of the attack. Performance became, in consequence of this, less vivid, devoid of subtle shading. The nineteenth century was the first time that someone of Chopin's distinction and mastery revolutionized the thought on the subject at hand. His students, interviewed by Michalowski and Kleczyński, rightfully dedicated their considerations mainly to the detailed process of the formation of his refined attack and his tone. The affirmations of Chopin's students on this point are the most authentic.

After beginning lessons, which dealt with exercises in the articulation of staccato, legato, portamento, and accentuated staccato, the method progressed to the easiest scales, presenting at the same time two fundamental hand positions.

"Chopin always began with the E major scale for the right hand, this being the easiest hand position. The left hand was taught for the first time with F-sharp major scale, this being the easiest position for the left hand."[19] The example shows both scales on one score, though naturally both would not have been played at the same time.

All methods in previous centuries had begun piano education in the C major scale, considered to be both the easiest position and the easiest scale. In Chopin's conception the C major scale was the most difficult scale. On this point it is necessary to introduce his view on the character of the fingers and to substantiate, not only this particular view, but also, the view on fingering and the entire process of his method.

The brief notes, planned to be a basis for his greater method, represent a document of unusual value, and will illustrate why Chopin used the E major scale as the easiest position, as the starting point of all playing; whereas other famous methods claimed that only the C major scale could be considered the easiest. This latter position is well represented in many methods: In Jean-Phillipe Rameau's C major "basic" five-finger position of the eighteenth century, which lasted through the nineteenth century; in Carl Czerny's systematic work on piano technique, continuing through Adolph Kullak's theoretical system in the late nineteenth century; and ending with the great Russian Piano School *Fortepiannaja igra* under the edition of A. Nikolajev, published in Moscow in 1977 and 1983.

The following fragment is a reaction of Chopin to the previous generation, and is cited in the short "Notizzen zur Méthode des Méthodes"[20]:

> Already it has been a long time that pianists have worked against nature, endeavoring to give fingers equal strength, when the opposite is the truth; each of the fingers has marked out for it a totally different role. The thumb has the greatest strength, for it is the thickest and is the most free finger [the most independent finger—*author*]. After the thumb follows the small finger opposite it. The main support of the hand is the middle finger [third finger], aided by the index or second finger. The weakest finger is the fourth one, in fact.[21]

Chopin is correct when he suggests that nobody takes into consideration the fact of unequal strength of the tones of the scale, stemming from the different build of each finger. So each finger should not be given the same strength, which is impossible and useless in Chopin's view; but instead, one should constantly think about the various strengths of the fingers commensurate with the construction of each, and should try to use this. Chopin ends with the assertion that the fifth finger is one of the weakest and also with trials to make the fourth finger independent from the third. As Chopin said, "There exist the various tones and the various fingers. The wit or ingenuity depends on benefitting from that variety. On that rests the art of fingering."[22] He apparently uses the longest fingers, which are further from the center of the wrist, for the black keys, and the shortest ones, the first and fifth, which are closer to the center of the wrist, for the white keys. Therefore he begins with the position in the E major scale, in the right hand, in which the properties of the fingers are recognized and used correctly.

He does likewise with the scale of F-sharp major in the left hand, in which the thumbs are on the white keys, so the shortest fingers are as near as possible to the key. Thus, the E major scale has fingering 1-2-3-4-1-2-3 and the F-sharp major scale has fingering 4-3-2-1-3-2-1.

Chopin, as can be seen, independently undertook those problems considered forever irrefutable, and for that reason, his views on fingering as well as his other innovations puzzled and sometimes annoyed his contemporaries. In the beginning, even such an authority as the famous pianist Fréderic Kalkbrenner took offense at Chopin's innovations and counseled Chopin to follow his lessons "for at least three years to correct these defects."[23]

Karol Mikuli demonstrated shocking differences in the fingering of the chromatic scale. Chopin's fingering was 4-3-4-3-4-5-3, etc., beginning with C, C-sharp, D, D-sharp, etc.[24] Here, Chopin used a manner of holding the hand on the keyboard totally different from his customary practice. Chopin's way is different from French fingering: 1-3-1-3-1-2-3, etc., and from the English fingering: 1-2-1-2-1-2-3, etc. Chopin's fingering is difficult and complicated, but provides a full-bodied, yet refined tone. Mikuli openly confessed that the fingering is connected with the individual style of the pianist's hand, with his individual creativity, and with the style of the technique, and for that reason he did not always use the hints of Chopin. In the edition of Chopin's works edited by Mikuli, there are certain deviations from the master's instructions. The original edition is by the Germany firm of Kistner.

The most useful example for explicating Chopin's view about crossing the longer fingers over the shorter ones is the Étude in A Minor, in which the chromatic scale is executed by the third, fourth, and fifth fingers of the right hand.

The next example illustrates Chopin's method of so much original fingering in the most impenetrable accompaniment. This method was unknown before him and shocked the pianists of his time, for it maintained the hand position in the same, "tranquil" form, even in the case of turning down the thumb after the fourth and fifth fingers—even on a black key!—or after crossing the fifth finger over the thumb (in opposite movement, downwards). The examples are from the Scherzo in B-flat Minor, the Étude in A Minor, Op. 25, and the Impromptu in A-flat Major, marked by asterisks in lines 2, 3, 4, 5, and 6.

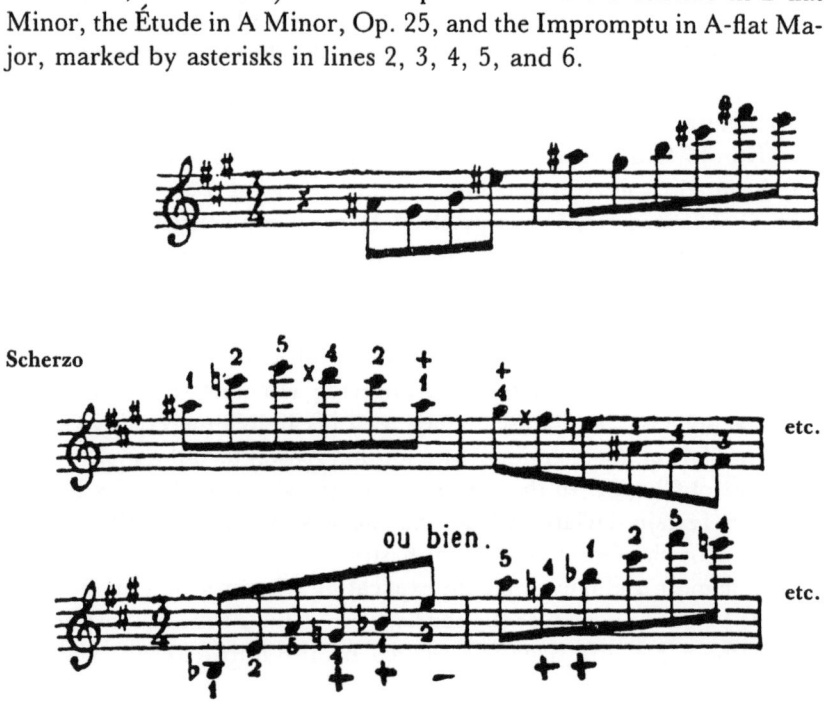

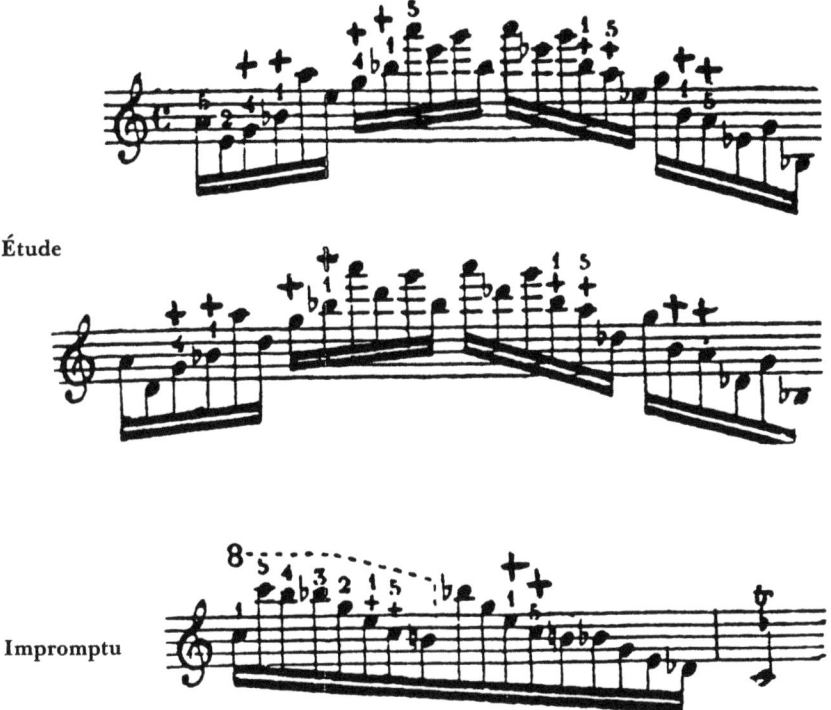

Étude

Impromptu

After this digression on the fingering in diatonic and chromatic scales, this study now returns to the method of Chopin, to the question of the independence of the fingers. Chopin differed from other teachers, not only in trying to refine the attack in the very first lessons, but also in his work on the diverse qualities of tone, by directing attention toward the liberty and independence of the fingers. As has been said before, in five-finger exercises he first recommended staying in slower tempos, still working on the independence of the fingers by the following means: "Let the fingers fall freely and lightly, and hold the hand as though suspended in air [weightless],"[25] signifying that the independence of the fingers should be established at the beginning of study, and not after long study, as a result of various exercises and études. This theory separates Chopin from other professors who were his contemporaries. For the same problem, the independence of the fingers, they continued by executing scales, accentuating each third or fourth note.

But, by further executing scales and passages also fortissimo and pianissimo, the quality of the tone thus came from the tone itself; and, thus, the hand would not be tired. The students of Chopin asserted to

Kleczyński that the frequent employment of the piano was intended to avoid *pesanteur* or "heaviness."

Every one of his pupils was obliged to play Chopin's favorite exercises, the second folder of his Préludes and the exercises by Muzio Clementi. Chopin valued Clementi's exercises highly, considering them beneficial for further development. The exercises in Chopin's method on the independence of the fingers and on the equality of tones had not been treated only mechanically, but with the presence of reason and will.

So far, the attack and the independence of the fingers have been discussed. In order to understand these subjects in Chopin's method, attention will now be turned to the position of the hand, which has already been mentioned above. The students of Chopin observed the hand of their master as "being sometimes held absolutely flat."[26] We can suppose that Chopin employed this manner in the singing tones or melodies. Thus, he avoided playing with the tips of the fingers, which gives more force and sureness to the fingers and the attack. The curved, rounded fingers also cause rapidity in play. And for this reason, this manner of the flat hand cannot be generalized as being present all of the time in Chopin's playing.

A consideration on his first position in the right hand will give the answer: It is more comfortable to have extended fingers, i.e., a flat hand in the position of E major—E, F-sharp, G-sharp, A, and B—than in the most difficult position, C major—C, D, E, F, and G. The C major position requires the fingers to be more in a "griff"; that is, in a more concentrated, curved position. This position is more suitable for strong and elastic tones, as well as for quick forté passages. The vigorously struck chord needs as absolutely concentrated hand, i.e., curved fingers. Chopin's hand position, though described as absolutely flat, was actually stretched; he simply had less curved fingers, using the pads of the fingers rather than the tips. Either method can be employed, depending on the nature of the executed sections. Chopin no doubt employed this manner occasionally, but his "flat" hand position has perhaps been somewhat exaggerated by his students.

In the field of *applicatura* or fingering, Chopin's new ideas were renounced by authorities in Paris from the beginning; but gradually these new ideas found their own audience and then were spread by students and carefully, even reverently, protected. From the time of J. S. Bach, a great reformer of keyboard rules, only Chopin audaciously overstepped the fingering rules by free application of the first finger on the black keys, when this procedure eased execution and helped maintain the "tranquility" of the hand and the evenness of the passages.

In another audacious departure, Chopin often employed the same finger for two successive notes; for instance, sliding the thumb from a black key onto a white key, or the fifth finger from a black key onto an adjacent white key. The execution was performed without the listener's perceiving the interruption between two tones. Further, he employed the "griff" of crossing the longer fingers over the shorter fingers, as shown in the example of Chopin's Étude in A Minor, (page 109), in the previous example cited, used in the most varied fingering for the situation.

The freedom and relaxation of our playing apparatus, for example in the beginning of the twentieth century, was the main premise in the theories of Steinhausen and Breihaupt. Now relaxation is the *sine qua non* in proper education in playing the piano. The other pioneering idea, that of singing legato playing, has been cultivated in our time as the basis of the Russian Piano School and remains so still. The leading of the hand, by fluid movement in scales and passages, distinguished Leszetycki's school at the turn of the twentieth century. The role of the mind and the will in participation during piano performance is again the chief topic of the theories of Leimer and Gieseking in the first three decades of the twentieth century.

Chopin can be acknowledged as a forerunner of many methodological thoughts, which other authors declared as their own, trying to seize them forever, writing voluminous treatises, carrying on propaganda on the styles of their teachings, and even searching in many instances for substantiation in scientific premises. Later in this text, in the discussion of Kullak's *Aesthetics,* the modern theories of pianistics are generally introduced, based on the results of the newer sciences, such as psychology, physiology, and acoustics, the results of which have been applied to the processes of piano playing.

The image of Chopin as a pedagogue should not remain in the shadow of Chopin the composer, today, especially when the interest of musicians and musicologists has turned to the intensive study and evaluation of all old, "obsolete" treatises.

REQUIRED REPERTOIRE AND CHOPIN'S LESSONS

The interpretation of music has been explained by Chopin in different works. Students gain charm, elasticity, and pliability in performance as a contrast to stiffness and numbness. They did not and should not dazzle the concert audience by their technique. The main aim always remained the truthful, convincing interpretation of ideas. The compositions commonly required by the master had been, as mentioned before, his Préludes and the exercises by Muzio Clementi as the first programmed task. Later, gradually, he assigned his pupils the more difficult Études and pieces by Moscheles and Bach.[27]

Before a concert Chopin played J. S. Bach's compositions exclusively. The independence of the fingers, the firm attack, and the *timbre* of the tone was most easily maintained by playing the preludes and fugues of J. S. Bach. The various *timbres* or tone colors and nuances occupied Chopin's mind throughout his entire life in teaching. "Good technique vies not to play everything by the same tone, but aspires to the refined attack and to the ultimate art of nuances."[28] Romanticism, as the new style of music, with its new aesthetics, pushed forward the requirements of *timbre* in opposition to the ideals of tonality embodied in Classicism. Chopin composed many of his pieces on the "black keys" (see his Études Op. 10 and Op. 25) in order to avoid the keys commonly used in the Classical era.

Later, when the requirements of "nice tone" were consolidated, students continued with less easy pieces, graded in order of difficulty; e.g., selected études from Cramer and Clementi (from *Gradus ad Parnassum*), suites and some fugues by Bach, nocturnes by Field and Chopin, then the sonatas of Mozart, Scarlatti, and Dussek, and solo pieces by the following composers: Händel, Hummel, Beethoven, Ries, Mendelssohn, Weber, Hiller, and Schumann. On the pieces of Field and Chopin, students were able to work out the deep, singing attack and to learn melodies that are to be played legato.

The lessons did not follow a mechanical pattern: exercises, études, small pieces for the purpose of studying a new interpretational problem, the repetition of compositions mastered before, polyphonic pieces intended to explain the contrapuntal technique, larger pieces like solo concertos, etc. Chopin liked variety in his lessons. "Sometimes he explained only; sometimes he sat behind the keyboard and showed how it needed to be played in order to satisfy his requirements."[29] The method of direct demonstration was probably used in the case of students with less capacity for musical imagination, inasmuch as this method has the greatest effect. Such an actual execution by a master must be remembered for one's whole life.

Chopin's "method of showing" can suggest that the students slavishly imitated the untouchable paradigm, the virtuosity of Chopin. In the previous paragraphs was mentioned the requirement of creative and fully conscious work, whether it was bound with phrasing or articulation or technique. In Mikuli's references, Chopin conscientiously fought against nonsensical practicing, willingly showing a "creative approach" toward any small problem.

Chopin, listening to the dull, unexpressive and colorless playing of his young artist, yelled: "Put all your soul there [in the music]! Play how you feel."[30] Chopin tried to stop any imitation of an artificial, wiseacre reasoning. He equally endeavored to cultivate the emotional and intellectual elements of playing. As it is known today, this is the only properly acceptable method of piano pedagogy. In addition the advice of the master often turned around thoroughly studied music theory. The sentence, "Play how you feel," probably also meant the omnipresent principle of the truth and simplicity of interpretation, as it is observed in Chopin's early works; for example, in both of his concertos for piano and orchestra. In Chopin's understanding it is the truthful playing which is truly captivating, in a certain sense "sincere," because one cannot play either convincingly or truthfully if he feels nothing. The emotionally inexperienced execution is nothing but dry structure. Art cannot be simply dead structure. The slogan can be converted into: "Not imitation, but creation." Thus, Chopin's method contradicts the methods of the "trained parrot" used in Paris. The sentence also hints that Chopin, even in his own works, allowed his students to deviate more or less from his own interpretational ideal.

Another meaning may be suggested for Chopin's sentence: It is a somewhat dangerous injunction for beginners, but a freeing moment for more mature students, since Chopin's effort was to give free passage to brain commands and the physiological realization by the fingers. The lack of psychic training and mental rigidity are the main hindrances to the well-felt and well-thought-out interpretation. The last known requirement, besides those mentioned before, was that students should participate in groups composed of good instrumentalists.[31] This advice was intended to encourage the aural imagination, the important psychic quality of future artists.

ON INTERPRETATION

In a search for questions regarding interpretation of Chopin's music, it is necessary to reconstruct the master's style and his views on "*tempo rubato* phrasing," rhythm, and pedaling. This, more than anything else except technique, contributes to the harmony of his performance.

First this statement must be mentioned: "Chopin played as the mood of the moment commanded him."[32] This undoubtedly shows Chopin's capacity for high inspiration and momentum; and the ability to transform his previously prepared, firm base into vibrant interpretation. This firm base allowed Chopin to deviate more or less, without deforming the contours of his original interpretational concept.

General opinion about Chopin's playing did not stabilize until 1900. As soon as Karol Mikuli published Chopin's works in Leipzig in 1879, intensive research on Chopin began. Mikuli confirms, in his preface to the 1879 Leipzig edition of Chopin's works, that Chopin still remained unknown as a pianist. However, according to Antoni Sygietyński (in Chopin's *Chronicle in Warsaw*), in addition to Marcelina Czartoryska and Karol Mikuli (who lived in Lvov, today a territory of the U.S.S.R.), there lived in Warsaw a third Polish student of Chopin. After a long search this authentic Polish student was found; he was ninety years old at that time. To Michalowski's question on how Chopin played the piano, the ninety-year-old student made this reply and nothing more: "Chopin played beautifully and charmingly."[33] This statement does not describe in any detail the delicate attack of the master, but rather addresses the complex whole, the beautiful harmony of all the elements in Chopin's interpretation.

Every scholar, musicologist, or pianist is eager to know more about Chopin's rubato. On this subject in particular, we have additional information. Tempo rubato is a powerful tool for the pianist, if used at the correct time and in the proper place. In fact, it has great significance in the interpretation of Chopin's compositions.

Rubato is not a device of Chopin exclusively. Certainly it existed, as is already well known, in the Gregorian chant before A.D. 1000, preserving the tradition of the declamations chanted by Greek bards. The sixteenth-century *recitative* in operas is actually the renaissance of the old traditions in Greek drama, and is actually in the rubato manner. The style passed into instrumental music; suggestions of it are in J. S. Bach's Chromatic Fantasy in D Minor or in the last sonatas of Beethoven (for example Adagio, Op. 106). Rubato began to be used more often; perhaps Chopin was the first who employed this style in his music with the most graceful manner. Already in the second movement of his Concerto in F Minor for piano and orchestra (in the introductory measures) the rubato is obvious. Later, Chopin employed it when the structure indicated the necessity. In many cases in his later works, Chopin did not write indicating rubato, but left the choice of rubato to the intelligence and the artistic taste of the interpreter.

Rubato in Chopin's Nocturne in C Minor (the end figuration in the right hand, as shown):

Marcelina Czartoryska, a student in the last couple of years of Chopin's life, provides richer information on the question of tempo rubato:

> Chopin did not ever exaggerate his fantasy, being guided by his outstanding aesthetic instinct. We are delivered from any exaggeration and false *pathos* by the simplicity of his poetic enthusiasm and moderation. The *rubato* of Chopin's rhythm liberated from all school bonds, but never passing into disharmony, nor anarchy.... To play Chopin without any rules, without *rubato*, veiling his accents ... we hear not Chopin, but his caricature. Chopin disdained over-sensitivity as false, and as a man educated in the music of J. S. Bach and Mozart, he could never seek capricious or exaggerated *tempi*. He would not stand for anything that could destroy the basic outlines of a composition; and, therefore, took care that students should not arbitrarily change *tempi*.[34]

This last sentence of Marcelina Czartoryska speaks about well-founded changes in tempo, logically called for by appropriate structures. Arbitrarily placed rubato irritated Chopin, as did uneven rhythmical playing (as mentioned before). Chopin did not understand *rubato* as a license for complete freedom, but rather as the expression of living agogics.

The author is obliged to acknowledge the efforts of Jan Ekier, the Polish pianist, professor of PWSM (Akademia Muzyczna Imeni Fryderyka Chopina) in Warsaw in the 1950s, in his new edition of Chopin's works. Ekier attempted to return the original, interpretational instructions to their rightful place, preferring intentional simplicity, retaining moderate use of rubato and so on, as a reaction to the abnormal, bloated state of interpretation characteristic of pianistics in the years before the First World War, when the dynamics and rubato tempi were overused. Accordingly, these personal remembrances of Czartoryska and Mikuli acquire particular importance.

In 1885, the great Polish pianist Alexander Michalowski visited the much older Karol Mikuli, who was the most respected authority on the problem of Chopinistic style, in Lvov. Mikuli had been a student of Chopin, as a twenty-three-year-old young man from the year

1844, when Chopin was at the peak of his fame. The lessons of an unknown pianist, at such a young age, with the most celebrated master in Europe must have left a deep imprint in Mikuli's memory. Michalowski acknowledged that Mikuli had a good memory, vividly preserving all the details of his studies.

One may rely on Mikuli's response to the question of Alexander Michalowski as to how Chopin comprehended rubato, since the resemblance to Czartoryska's observations is evident:

> Chopin widely employed *rubato* in his playing, and he was far from rigorous metrically, accelerating or slowing down this or that motive.... But for each *rubato* Chopin had an unshakable emotional logic.... It interpreted itself by the intensification and slowing down of the melody, by the details of the harmony, by the construction of the figuration. It was fluent, natural, and never fell into exaggeration or affectation.[35]

The rubato was understood and employed by Chopin, surely, as the result of considerable reflection. The rubato which "never fell into anarchy" is confirmed by Mikuli as a most objective description. Mikuli says that Chopin "in the right hand, in the melody, and in the arabesques, allowed for a great liberty; but in the left hand, held to the exact *tempo*."[36] The contemporary interpretational style of Chopin's works is entirely commensurate with that mentioned by Mikuli.

It was Mozart who first said, "Let our left hand be our leader and let it always hold to the *tempo*." Is this not the first undefined notion of rubato? As Chopin himself proclaimed, "The left hand, it is the director of the orchestra."[37] One English critic was the first to write favorably about Chopin's rubato: "Chopin knows to move freely in his bars."[38] Otherwise, Berlioz and others, such as Meyerbeer, did not accept "the novelty" of Chopin.

At that time rubato was considered among musical classicists or purists to be in violation of the firm measure. Berlioz swore that Chopin did not know how to hold the tempo. Liszt interpreted Chopin's rubato poetically, stating: "The foliage is rocking in the wind and life is awakening and developing in it, but the tree unmoved stands in its own place."[39] So carefully did Chopin incorporate the question of rubato into the minds and habits of his students, that they preserved and carried it into the next generation.

Liszt left behind interesting and striking wisdom as an aid to fine execution: "All compositions of Chopin must be played while observing the rules of accentuation and prosody, but with a certain excitement, the secret of which is difficult to discern for one who has not heard the master."[40] The agitation, "the excitement," is poetic veiling of the rubato, because the first phase of rubato is in fact an exciting accelerando, set after a few vague notes at the beginning, reaching a culmination, and ending with release; then a small ritardando, the second phase of rubato. "The secret" probably means the way in which the proportion among these separate phases was balanced. The proportion is in fact unprescribable exactly; inasmuch as each phrase or figure in music can have a different "proportion," the rubato is different also.

ON PHRASING

In the interpretation of music, and especially Chopin's music, it is also important to be acquainted with Chopin's principles on making the pronunciation of the musical phrase, i.e., musical thoughts, more distinctive. In spoken language we know exactly how to use punctuation. Principal and subordinate sentences are clearly indicated by commas. More precise explanations in the text are set off by parentheses or brackets. Often we underline certain sentences or special terms in the text in order to make them more visible, stressing their significance. Musical phrasing has similar characteristics. Each epoch develops a new type of musical speech. New types of motives or phrases (short, longer, or of unexpected length) are shaped by the structure of the music. In the early works of Chopin, simplicity of expression is found, especially considering that his style is far from any affectation or overly rapid changes in movement. Chopin's ornamentation is an organic part of the melody.

In the interpretation of his works, one should think constantly about this unity between the principal idea (melody) and the lace (ornamental, small notes). If the ornaments are executed heavily or inappropriately, with the same importance as the main motive, in the same tempo as the structure before, then they produce banality, spoiling the formal perfection of Chopin's music.

The small groupings of notes (grupetti) and other types of ornaments in Chopin's works appear often for the first time in a simple way, together with the melody. The motives are repeated in the next variations with more elaborate ornaments, requiring a certain deceleration at the beginning of the ornamentation and an accelerando at its end. Properly translated: The ornamentation needs the tempo rubato. A glance through Chopin's nocturnes or waltzes will enable one to see the various examples of rich ornamentation.

Kleczyński recollects how Chopin made a comparison between two types of speech: "In spoken language, one does not pronounce the chief thought and the incidental ones with the same importance; the incidental thoughts are in the shadow, and rightly so."[41] The analogy between music and language is how Chopin expressed his view of necessary separation of different phrases, different nuances of the forte and the piano (even in the smallest motives). Usually the musical phrase is composed of eight measures. The interpreter should properly show the termination of the musical thought (theme). Chopin indicated this by a period and by the statement, "... let us pause slightly and lower the voice."[42] The secondary division of this phrase, i.e., the smaller units (four or twice two), needs a shorter stop, marked by Chopin as a comma, or else a semicolon. Without these important stops, the punctuation changes into chaos. The Chopin Waltz in A-flat Minor, Op. 69, shows the proper detachment of measures divided into two bars with the most stressed as the longest tone of the phrase (see the second example). First the piece as written by Chopin:

Kleczyński shows how Chopin executed this piece:[43]

and finally, by incorrect accentuation, the whole phrase and with it the sense of music can be comically mutilated:

The + sign indicates the terminal note of each second measure. These terminal notes should be excused as shorter and weaker notes (as in the example of how Chopin executed his waltz).

From many general rules of phrasing, Chopin came to the final conclusion, and he pursued it firmly: "Do not play by too small a phrase"[44]; ultimately meaning, do not subdivide the music into minute elements of musical thought, because then the musical process drags, slows down, and becomes tiring. Chopin's advice can be understood as singing in long phrases, avoiding small and short parts as much as possible. Included here is his Scherzo in B-flat Minor, the right hand without accompaniment:

Each eighth measure has been detached, as the long phrasing sign shows, and also has Chopin's "agogic apostrophes." In fact, the last or fourth line has the significant detachment by Chopin's "semicolon." This denotes the end of the phrase in spoken language. This melody seems to be unlimited. In the example accentuation is not often employed. Chopin also sought support for his theory in rules of singing, which could be perfected by listening to good singers.

The problem with phrasing begins with superimposing of the arc sign above the musical phrase, signifying legato playing. Chopin tried to remove the vagueness from the commonly adopted system. He suggested and marked for his students the diverse members of the phrase by commas, semicolons, and dots.[45] In addition to all of this, execution with long phrases is connected to Chopin's method of "singing legato," which was the object of special studies in Chopin's lessons. His compositions speak significantly about his ability to express himself by means of broadly based musical thoughts. In the introduced example of his Waltz in A-flat Minor, the construction of the composition shows the prevalance of short motives.

Chopin's intention was to overarch, as much as possible, a mere construction by interpretation, with as long a breadth as possible.[46] Later, in the discussion of Lussy, one will find Chopin's deliberations on phrasing, under the name of Lussy, as a significant contribution to the phrasing in his century.

PEDALING

This topic was researched much less in the nineteenth century than it has been in the twentieth. The German theorist Martienssen, a professor of the University of Berlin, variously in 1930, 1937, and 1954, first revealed the role of the aural imagination, originating in our inner ear, and the role of the will, "Gestaltungswille," as a *spiritus movens* or "driving force" of the interpretational art, and of our technique. The aural imagination has various functions which tell one about the character of each sound received from an instrument or about the pulsating rhythm in these lines.

The creation of individually colorized tones and tone complexes (more lines) on the piano is considerably complicated by pedaling. Martienssen categorized the three functions of the pedal as (1) acoustic, (2) connecting, and (3) harmonic[47] for the various purposes of sound changes. The achievement of nice, round, and full tone, legato playing and the prolongation of tones so that one may hear their accord, are the main roles of pedaling as Martienssen describes them.

When Chopin penetrated into the secret of legato playing, he also penetrated the secret of pedaling. Before studying the employment of the pedal in Chopin's works, it should be noted that: (1) the indications of pedaling in editions are sometimes incorrect (Gliński and Kleczyński call attention to this)[48]; and (2) the usage of the pedal is in many instances individual, and cannot be prescribed by precise rules. Artists continually develop and discover new effects of the pedal. They are also dependent on the instrument and the acoustics of the place where the execution occurs. However, the most frequent situations encountered in Chopin's volumes of études, nocturnes, concerti, and preludes have been selected. Each employment of the forte pedal is indispensable:

1) In broken chords and processes when the tones are not changed. The passages in which the harmony sounds beautiful should be frequently pedaled (as in the example of the Étude in A-flat Major, Op. 25, No. 1). This is Chopin's speciality:

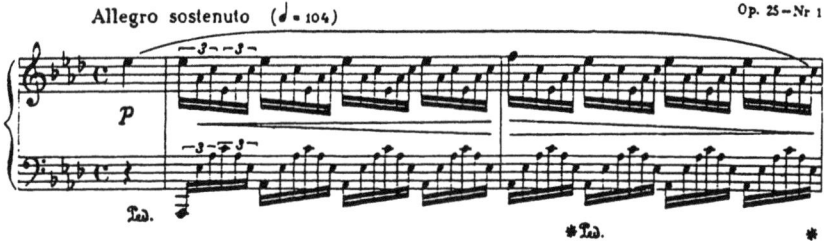

2) The same hand, executing melody and the accompaniment, needs pedaling in order to distinguish the singing melody. This effect also became more frequent in Liszt's works, such as his Nocturnes, as well as Thalberg's solo pieces. The example is from Chopin's Étude No. 5, Op. 25, the trio:

3) In large crescendos the instrument must have a forceful sonority, raised sometimes to prodigious proportions; for example, in Chopin's Polonaise in A-flat Major, Op. 53, in the trio with octaves.

4) Chopin augmented the beauty and richness of the tone with the pedal, without consciously introducing with the principal tone, especially in the middle part of the keyboard. It is necessary to avoid not only the mixture of neighboring notes, thus producing dissonances; but also the two notes belonging to the same consonant chord. In Chopin's Nocturne, Op. 15, No. 2 in F-sharp major, the first measure demonstrates both cases mentioned above:

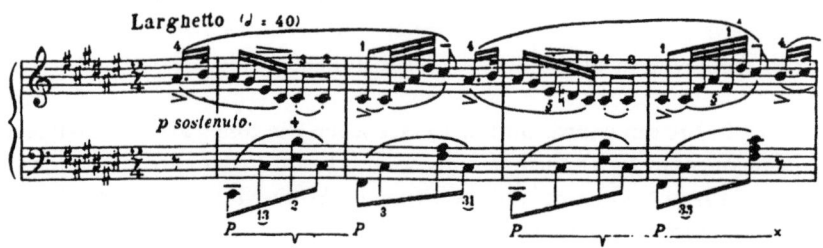

5) The upper octaves of the piano admit to more frequent and longer usage of the pedal than the middle octaves of the keyboard.

6) "Chopin used the pedal often for supporting certain notes of the singing melody, in such a way that he pressed the pedal after striking the note."[49] Today this is called the "syncopated pedal." Using it, one can obtain considerable legato between successive chords. The example is from Chopin's Nocturne in G Minor, Op. 37, No. 1, the middle part:

The indication of the pedal at the left, below the grand staff, shows the delayed or syncopated pedal by note on the special line. The right side shows the continuation of the piece. A similar example is in Chopin's Sonata in B-flat Minor, Op. 35, in the third movement, *Marche funèbre*, in which can be recognized the sound of bells. A very short abandonment of the pedal is used for avoiding dissonance, usually to separate heavy, dissonant chords, as in Chopin's Scherzo No. 1, in the introduction:

Chopin pushed toward perfection a combination of the forte pedal and piano pedal. His ornamented fioritures sound delicate and beautiful with pedals simultaneously depressed. In the Concerto in F Minor, the Larghetto would be impossible without such a treatment, as would the Nocturnes. Kleczyński maintains that "Chopin passed often unnoticed from the forte pedal to the left pedal, mainly in enharmonic modulations."[50] These passages must have had particular charm in Chopin's execution, since on today's pianos they are said to be an object of instant experience, typically hedonism and fascination. The subject of the left pedal should be discussed in more detail. Even if the effects of the left pedal are enchanting, one must be aware of its overuse. Many passages are supposed to be executed simply and without pedaling, as in Chopin's Nocturne in F Major, Op. 15 (first part), or *Andante Spianato*, Op. 22, the middle part in 3/4 time.

CONCLUSION

Above all the other elements in the execution of music, in particular Chopin's music, is a crown called intelligence, the essential judge of faithful interpretation. It is not enough that an interpreter plays in harmony with his emotions or his enthusiasm; he is obliged to interpret the composer, to execute the composition as the composer understood and intended it. To remain faithful to the composer's intention means to penetrate the thoughts, intentions, and feelings of the composer; for this, one needs intelligence.

Several years after Chopin's death, Professor Stanislaw Tarnowski, a well-known historian of Polish literature, recollected his conversations with Marcelina Czartoryska. He asked her what she regarded as the main condition for "cultivated execution." Her reply was:

> Intelligence . . . true intelligence comprises emotions, sometimes even zeal and execution lie in them, as they lie in it. The interpreter is obliged

not to think about himself at all, to forget himself entirely, and to adapt his playing to the mind, feelings, and style of the composer, in order to play and to evoke each shade of mind, fantasy, and sensation of the Haydn or Mozart, whom he, in fact, is interpreting.[51]

The recollections of Czartoryska were undoubtedly inspired by her master's style of teaching and thinking. Without this quality Chopin would not have been able to capture the whole cultural world of Europe.

To summarize the contribution of Chopin means first to acknowledge his intuitive talent in order to penetrate, not only into the substance of the music itself, into the new piano music, but also into piano pedagogy problems. As a man of genius, Chopin boldly changed the rules of his musical heritage. Today's pianistics owe him much for many new ideas, which after his death and later, became the assumptions of the new methods in piano performance.

Franz Liszt

Franz (Férenc) Liszt did not leave behind any methodological work on the piano, although he educated a multitude of famous pianists such as von Bülow, Tausig, D'Albert, Rosenthal, Klindworth, and many others. Liszt's life was considerably longer than Chopin's; therefore, Liszt's pedagogical activity forms a richer picture. Liszt was active in several cultural centers of Europe—Paris, Weimar, Rome, Budapest, and Geneva—not only as a pedagogue of piano, but also as a composer. He also had a full life as a concert pianist throughout Europe, including the European part of Russia. Unfortunately we do not possess any authoritative source of information that is objective on his teaching in Weimar, where he spent two long periods of his life. In Weimar at that time, there existed a significant school of virtuosos.

The results of Liszt's teaching in Paris have been captured in the form of a diary of Augusta Boissier. She noted the course of each lesson given to her daughter. Liszt was young, hardly twenty-one years old, so that his image here as a pedagogue does not have the scope of an experienced, mature pianist and composer of great style, such as he was in Budapest, near the end of his life. Nevertheless, this diary by Mme. Boissier, who was originally from Geneva, attracts us with its immediateness. The original was written in French; the translations provided in this work, however, are into English from the German translation *Franz Liszt als Lehrer,* published in 1930.

Augusta Boissier encountered Liszt in Paris. Charmed by his execution, she entrusted him with her daughter. She herself listened to each lesson and had no lack of observational talent, for sometimes we have the impression of standing directly before Liszt when he was teaching.

In order to characterize the posture of Liszt as a pedagogue, this work will start with the first lessons as noted in Augusta Boissier's diary. From her journals a unique look at the problems of piano technique can be gained; other sources do not speak of piano craft as meticulously as Augusta Boissier.

The first lessons of the young Liszt began with the field of technical training. In many instances these lessons are reminiscent of the school of Carl Czerny, instructing young piano students through the five-finger exercises, executed in all keys, in chromatic succession. The mechanical training of individual fingers in Liszt's "method" takes long practice daily.[52] "The fingers are lifted high so that the tone is as a result full."[53]

FINGERS AND ATTACK

How did Liszt treat the problem of the attack and the positioning of the fingers? The fingers which are not playing lie motionless on the keys; meanwhile, the finger playing attacks the key with strength, ". . . kraftig Anschlage während die übrigen unbeweglich bleiben. . . ."[54] The fingers should play independently, literally, "with rounded and totally equal fingers."[55] The third, fourth, and fifth fingers are, in the opinion of Liszt, the worst fingers. Liszt's view differs from that of Chopin, who considers the third and fifth to be the best fingers.

The instructions for Boissier's daughter continue in detail as to each finger, following the next pattern: "Each finger must be lifted up very high and laid down on the pad of the finger."[56] One can even read while playing. Chopin decidedly rejected this element of distraction; moreover, in his lessons, one had to be aware each moment of his movements on the keyboard. But this method of reading while playing was used commonly in Paris, for example, by Kalkbrenner's students and others.

The attack of the fingers is responsible for the tone quality, and is taught in the beginning because of the desirability of this technique: At first one plays each note slowly, with the pad, and not the tip of the finger, with the hand "more stretched" than rounded.[57] This type of attack produces a naturalness and lightness of playing. It is also the method of Moscheles, the most prominent representative of the great European piano school in Leipzig in the second half of the nineteenth century.

WRIST

Except for practicing the attack, the work of the wrist is no less important. On this point the observations of Boissier seem to reveal Liszt's instructions as less inventive than those of Chopin: "The tone is clear, full, round, and completed, not stifled and small. One must play fully from the wrist without exception...,"[58] leaving the arm motionless; "as if through an elastic motion, the hand has fallen from the wrist on each note."[59] Chopin's hand and arm are free, but Liszt's student plays from the beginning with the wrist only, with the arm motionless. The whole apparatus is not loosened as in Chopin's "method."

In the other lesson, Liszt's attack is done as Boissier states: "...with full and soft attack from the wrist throughout. His fingers have no bones nor nerves; they are soft paws, even in the powerful *forti.*"[60] Fingers are not glued to the keyboard, neither as in J. S. Bach's execution, nor as in Chopin's method.

The thumb and the third fingers are carefully drilled at the beginning of the education, these being "the essential fingers and points of support of the hand."[61] The other fingers are secondary, and after careful and sufficient exercise of them, the secondary fingers are treated equally "until an even attack is reached."[62]

When Liszt encountered an incapable finger in playing piano music, he lingered at that detail and did not play the entire piece. This quotation from page 105 of Augusta Boissier's diary gives a clear picture of the fingers' positions during Liszt's playing: "There is no definite form to the way he holds his fingers. They are soft and flexible or 'weich und geschmeidig,' in every sense supple or 'biegsam,' and they drag from one key to another." In the notes from the seventh lesson, January 15, 1832, Augusta Boissier treats the same question once more:

> Liszt does not hold the fingers rounded, because it gives a certain dryness to the execution, which he cannot bear; but on the other hand, one cannot say that his fingers lie flat on the keyboard. They are mobile and elastic ['die Geschmeidigkeit'], so that they do not keep any precisely describable position, attacking the keys in all ways, without exception, which causes unstiff and non-dry play."[63]

Later, in the description of Liszt's considerably controversial hand positioning, as observed by his students, critics, and writers, acknowledgment of the full debt to Augusta Boissier's keen observations will be given.

TECHNICAL EXERCISES

As in Chopin's "method," the hands and scales should be practiced separately and especially slowly, in "three or four keys, one hour daily, then in countermovement in all of the keys, as well as in broken chords, and in the full chord, 'C-E-G-C,' from the lowest octave to the highest, and in the opposite way."[64] This information on the single tones and scales is amazingly not placed at the end of the book, but in the "method" figure in the first place. The following exercises are recommended as a daily obligatory item:

(left hand in the same way)

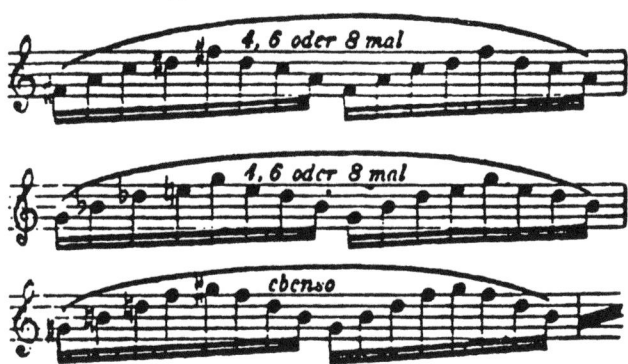

As Boissier tells more and more about each moment of her daughter's lessons, one becomes more interested in and captivated by the details of the process of an artist at work. The figures shown above should be played either four, six, or eight times with free, totally even fingers, and legato (in the original: "mit verbundenen Fingern").[65] In connection with this, Boissier's daughter was instructed to work on dynamics systematically, starting with a delicate, soft piano and coming up to full fortissimo strength. Liszt compiled a series of crescendo and decrescendo studies for her, and advised her to make up her own dynamic combinations. As an example of similar patterns the following can be used:

The example from page 129 is executed with dynamics also, first slowly with uniform fingers; then more quickly when mastered thoroughly; and finally, with both hands simultaneously, through all of the chromatic keys.

THE PRINCIPLE OF FLEXIBILITY

Most important to understand is Liszt's intention to give both the fingers and the hand the greatest possible flexibility and pliability. Liszt stressed many times, as can be witnessed in many places in Boissier's journals, that all joints of the hand, including the knuckles of the fingers, should be elastic. Liszt's hand has been described as being "in constant motion on the piano, without any curvature, rocking itself in freedom and charm."[66] Without a doubt, the training materials he gave to the student Liszt himself had played at a very young age, in a way that each note was attacked from the wrist. He addressed each note separately and meticulously. Liszt, like Chopin, also used the method of demonstration, playing fragments or whole pieces for his students.

The lessons continued by developing the "pliable" hand and "independent and energetic fingers," by playing octaves with the same repeated note, which later had to be accelerated; so Boissier informs us in the eighth lesson, January 16th.[67] The octaves and the broken octaves are executed in chromatic sequence in all scales, including the parallel minor scales:

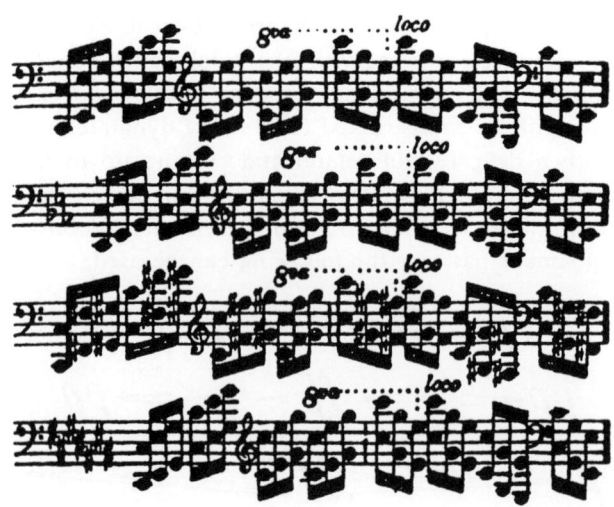

Furthermore the drill to develop pliable and energetic fingers enables the student to play more chords on the same note; and again, the drill on the same note enabled a row of trills for certain fingers; meanwhile, the idle fingers are held motionless on the keys. "At the end of this series the individually attacked notes are played again ... as the other fingers remaining motionless on the keys."[68] The octaves required by Liszt should be executed afterwards, also with equally soft, yet rebouncing wrist, for hours at a time.

Weitzmann gives the exact fingering for trills in certain passages in his interpretation of Liszt's compositions:

> Liszt executed the tone rows sharply with the stronger second finger out, and the same octave row with the first and third or first and fourth fingers. In a longer or stronger trill, he used not only the closest fingers, but also those more distant from each other; such as the first and third fingers, or the third and the fifth. So the right hand executes the trill by the following fingering: 1-4-2-3.[69]

In today's understanding, this new fingering of Liszt's startles nobody; but in his day it was something unusual, like the fingering of his contemporary, Chopin.

Among the many types of exercises which Liszt considered most important for the development of piano technique, we also find the seventh chords in all keys and the diminished sevenths, played *ad aeternum,* the thirds played with both hands as scales (Chopin recommended Zimmerman's exercises), and finally the thirds, diminished and chromatic with both hands together, ending with scales in sixths.[70] Once again, Liszt required that all of these exercises be played with the same evenness of the fingers. When Liszt practiced, he did gymnastics of the hand for "at least two hours daily, and after all the exercises, he advised one to play the scales strongly and quickly."[71] The pianistic art is based upon sacrifice, sometimes even to the point of self-denial. The myth that talent can overcome everything is dissolved after reading Mme. Boissier's tiny book.

Staccato and legato have been considered by the most compelling virtuosos of the past century as the two most important ingredients of interpretation. Staccato articulation is often found in music, and certainly in Liszt's music as well. Liszt let his students play many études with staccatoed octaves, and on one occasion was provoked to say: "Have patience with yourself,"[72] otherwise the result will not come. Compare the observation: "...his trills are equal like pearls ... the thirds as well as the sixths of the piece are of perfect evenness. No one note is less strong than the other one. Both fingers strike well and at the same time ... so that the sound is only one.... Nowhere can one perceive the fatigue and the effort.... The octave passages are executed with marvellous lightness."[73] The following fragment, remarking on Liszt's playing of an étude of Moscheles, states something more: "... his bass is simultaneously bound [legato or connected], rhythmicized, measured ... but not one hard or abrupt note. Each nuance is justified, studied, and thought over."[74]

LOGICAL ELEMENT

Since Liszt logically justified each detail in his own playing, similarly he allowed each of his students to justify individual requirements, which Liszt introduced during his pupil's lessons. More detailed reflection should be given to the fact that Liszt had a broader approach to the study of piano. Liszt insisted on the study of the music theory of the famous Czech professor in Paris, the composer Antonín Rejcha. Other evidence lies in Liszt's advice to study modulations and to transpose études into various keys, with more elaborate harmonization; Liszt believed this belonged to the foundations of musical art and promised great future achievements.

Because Liszt's "method" is as well organized as his thoughts and ideas, and because he can trace all problems back to their primary origin, his views are certain and correct, an opinion confirmed in the following statements. "He leads all music toward its origin, even if he has marked out everything in the music precisely. I find Liszt to be logical and original to the utmost, because he never exaggerates and is not prejudiced."[75] The remarks are meant to apply, not only narrowly to the domain of Liszt's technique, but also to his solution of interpretational issues. Liszt as a pedagogue had a primary principle: To give the student freedom of action, but to reign in any willfulness. Throughout Boissier's journals can be found similar sentences, expressing the author's admiration of Liszt's style of teaching. In order to round out this chapter on pianistic technique, the following quotations on Liszt are provided: "He seems to have an endless, meditative depth; his mind is that of a thinker."[76] "All the conventional rules which have been valid in music until now, he sweeps away."[77] "The descant sang purely ... and ... full of spirit ... the feeling were fine ... of fastidious art, as if something other than music should be rendered."[78]

SYNOPSIS OF LISZT'S TEACHING TECHNIQUE

Liszt's postulate as a pedagogue was to lead each student individually, so that his method would not educate all students according to the same mold. He avoided mechanical drilling of his students by various shadings of dynamics and the art of a natural, pliable, round tone. He developed the musical intellect from the very beginning, even in very young students, by requiring precise observation and differentiation of musical phenomena. For his own part, Liszt attempted logically to justify his own idiosyncrasies in his performances, and he required that his students do the same.

Liszt did not leave a thorough, organized description of his teaching method. However, when one considers Liszt's various renditions and critiques of his interpretations, drawn from practically all the musical centers of Europe, one can obtain a complex picture of his artistic prominence. These sources allow the conclusion that there is a relationship between his teaching methods and his multi-leveled, perennially mutable art. Liszt seemed to be able to transform himself into many incarnations, but he never lost his individuality.

This feature of Liszt's distinctive interpretation of each composer and each piece seems to have logical ties with his ability to deal individually with each of his students. The famous Hans von Bronsart, a student of Liszt, wrote in 1854: "Liszt led everyone according to his specific and individual qualities; Liszt's ability to recognize these qualities with sureness was the most unusual feature of his genius."[79]

To enrich the image of Liszt's method of teaching, attention will be focused toward the process of learning a musical piece as Liszt approached it.

LISZT'S APPROACH TO LEARNING THE MUSICAL PIECE

Boissier, depicting as she did each lesson conducted by the young Liszt, inevitably included questions connected with learning new pieces. This topic eventually became the subject of long debates in contemporary methods, such as that of the Russian author Arsenij Shchapov in his *Fortepiannyj urok v muzykalnoj shkole i uchilishche* (The Piano Lesson in the Conservatory and Academia), Moscow, 1947. Liszt's mode of penetrating an unknown composition is highly instructive, as well as captivating. Boissier's observations omitted no part of the learning process, which can be divided into:

1) musical notes, their values, and pauses;

2) observation of the dynamics of a piece;

3) understanding of the musical space, that is, of the first and most important stratum of the composition, that which is first heard in execution: thematic lines, important basses, and important accents;

4) the less important strata of piano structure, the non-thematic and complementary sounds;

5) the stabilizing of the final tempo, giving the proper character to the piece, then the shading of the accelerando and ritardando segments; and

7) the memorization of the piece and, consequently, the mastery of any technical pianistic problems.

Taking in hand the composition that he intended to learn, Liszt proceeded as follows:

> He began, not casually, with a common reading or overview; but rather, penetratingly investigated the text of the piece. He played it slowly and very attentively, four or five times. On the first time through, he only attempted to play all of the notes as they were written, adding nothing, and omitting nothing. During the second time, Liszt followed the value of the notes, the pauses and the dotted rhythms, with scrupulous precision, not allowing himself the slightest deviation. For the third time, Liszt observed the *forti, piani,* accents, *crescendi,* in a word, all of the given dynamic shading in the text, to which Liszt then added interpretively. Liszt assumed it was necessary to add some interpretational signs, as he was of the opinion that composers treated this matter with some carelessness. In this step, he took care to give the most appropriate expression to each detail of the dynamics; sometimes attempting many different techniques and combinations until he was satisfied that the dynamics expressed the inner content of the piece. On his fourth time through a new piece, Liszt would turn his attention to the proper relationship between the bass and the melody; and then to discovering the melodic figurations of the individual voices in order to stress the important elements and to de-emphasize the accompanying voice. During the fifth time through, he deliberated on the question of *tempo,* adapting and subordinating it to the character of the composition, slowing down or accelerating according to the expression of each phrase. Liszt allows this only in music which requires it; but not in certain works of Classicism, nor in fugues. Only after this involved process of fundamental realization of the basic elements of a musical piece, did Liszt commit a musical piece to memory and pursue its technical mastery.[80]

Boissier was evidently fascinated by the secret of Liszt's "reading" of a new piece, and she gave a praiseworthy account of this process. She did not, however, enumerate the problems confronting an interpreter that require considerable deliberation even before he commences work on a piece. There are undoubtedly more than she has enumerated here. Fingering, articulation, and phrasing all have important roles. On these points Boissier's account does not satisfy us today. However, one finds the value of this fragment lies, not necessarily in its account of the number of questions which intrigued Liszt and why they did so; but rather, perhaps, in the image it gives one of the breadth and penetration of Liszt's approach to a new piece. The thoroughness of this initial analysis, on which Liszt insisted, is recognized by any twentieth-century pianistic school as a prerequisite for any new repertoire. Liszt emphasized the importance of this principle a hundred years before the methodologists of the twentieth century became involved with it.

LISZT'S PERFORMANCE: EXPRESSION

During the most prolific years of Liszt's triumphant concert tours through Europe, the term "Lisztomania" originated, certainly trying to capture the magnetic charm of his performance. Liszt was called "the Paganini of the piano" which he liked; and it was not untrue. Yet it is imperative to distinguish between the "two Paganinis." "As for Liszt, his rendition was based upon a command of the entire field of his musical art, that is of all forms of composition. From this entirety the virtuoso appears; this is not Paganini, who only achieves virtuosity."[81] This statement was written in 1860 by Liszt's most significant student and ardent follower, concert pianist, Carl Tausig (1841–1871). Liszt was forty-nine years old, and the characteristics of his playing had stabilized. Tausig openly said that Liszt's mystery lay in his expression. Similarly, Tausig accurately writes: "I said to myself that I am not standing above the difficulties in the Don Juan Fantasy (Liszt's virtuoso piano composition), I have difficulties; only he is standing above it, only he."[82] Probably the expression Liszt is able to give to his piece is why he stands "above."

Technique was only a tool for the expression of Liszt's nuanced feelings and thoughts, never his objective. When one asks scientifically what the substance of Liszt's performance is, one needs to go deeper into the process of molding the sound structure which makes the interpreter more than a performer of something which was created before him. The performer/interpreter must equally attempt creation by himself, if he has something of his own to say. A famous excerpt from reviews of Liszt's time represents d'Ortique's understanding of Liszt's creative talent and expression. This is excerpted from the "Gazette musicale de Paris," published in 1834, when Liszt was only twenty-three years old. The critique starts, neither from single enumeration of the individual pieces, nor from the technique; but from trying directly to capture the most interesting feature of the young virtuoso.

> His interpretation is his speech, his soul. He is the most poetic, perfect summary ['Inbegriff' in the original] of all expressions.... These expressions are delivered in clear and determinate thoughts which he reproduced in complete limitlessness with the strength of truthfulness... with energy of feelings with a spell of charm, never before achieved. He speaks, his art is an organ which he uses for developing his ideas. From this we see that Liszt's interpretation is no mechanical or material exercise, but much more; and in a proper sense it is composition, the real creation of art.[83]

As a creative person, Liszt was able to find inspiration everywhere—in landscape, in literature, in history, in any given moment of life. He undoubtedly had an unlimited potential for fiendish difficulty and lyricism. He did not trust the well-trod pathways.

Liszt's years of concert activity led Schumann to put down in writing the elusive moments of Liszt's rendition. Schumann discusses the sound changes which the instrument underwent through Liszt's treatment. He speaks of Liszt's style of attack on the keyboard, and of Liszt's mode of changing position of the hands. However, Schumann speaks about more than merely technical points; he discusses the high ethical level of the artist in words that are not easy to translate: "The instrument blazes and sparkles in the hands of its master ... it is no longer piano performance of this or that sort, but the speech of a bold character. He triumphs over skill and the danger of the tool and renders the serenity of art."[84] In the Romantic period of the nineteenth century, art was usually evaluated through the prismatic categories of the poetic or the fantastic, and then through the "less romantic" categories. As a man of this era, Schumann highlighted these aspects of Liszt's performance, the attribute usually called by the common but apt name of dramaticism—which, as a category of aesthetics, stayed lower in the hierarchy of German aesthetics, affected as it was by Hegel's system of thought.

As the examination of Liszt's performances continues, one other important source must be mentioned: Liszt's former student, the chamber music virtuoso and professor Laura Rappoldi-Kahler. In her letters she expressed to Julius Kapp observations similar to those of Schumann. For instance, she categorically describes the transformations of quality of piano sound during Liszt's renditions. Rappoldi's analysis is original, yet objective; she judges Liszt's various fingerings and hand positions, as well as his attacks. Her analysis offers an objective basis for comparison, as presented below. This analysis was written in 1870, five years before Liszt's death.

> I have been listening to Liszt's playing daily, often for several hours. First Liszt played Bach and then Scarlatti. The piano [das Klavier] seemed like an organ to me, in the style of Bach. Liszt played Bach amazingly slowly. Today no one can stand to hear such a performance! With Scarlatti the pieces gave the impression of being played on a harpsichord of the past century, and yet it was still the Bechstein piano on which we all had been playing. Liszt gave the impression that we were hearing an entirely different instrument. What struck me was that somehow Liszt "orchestrated" with his fingers; and in most of his works, particularly in his Rhapsodies, Liszt developed astonishing and never-before-heard splendors of tone-color. His execution was poetry, was expression.[85]

Thanks to this observation, one can infer that Liszt was able to control all the detailed movements of his fingers in the highest degree, thus differentiating each shade of sound. Liszt was aware of the slightest movements of his joints and had the ability to relax them instantaneously. On these processes depend the strength and color of his tone—what is called the "fine attack." Here Rappoldi addresses one of the most delicate questions of artistic performance, Liszt's sensibility for *timbre*.

Regarding Liszt's hand positioning, Rappoldi notes that in order to produce the sound he desired, Liszt performed "each composer . . . even each different piece, with fingers and hands positioned differently."[86] This observation stops all contradictory views on the subject of Liszt's hand positioning.

Finally, Rappoldi agrees entirely on the importance of the individuality, the creative powers, and what is fantastic in Liszt's interpretation: "While Rubinstein was playing, for instance, one could listen to the instrument, his playing was always and remained a marvellous piano rendition. When Liszt played, one did not hear the instrument; but rather heard him, and followed his tones, his intense fantasy, which he imprinted on every musical work as the stamp of his own creation."[87]

About the playing of this fascinating pianist, other references are available giving other impressions similar to Rappoldi's. A composer and year-long friend of Liszt, Felix Draeseke, writes about him thus:

> I cannot compare his performance with those of other virtuosos, and I have the impression that the piece is rising only under his hands and

gives the impression of artistic improvisation ... and it can happen that in another performance that the same piece appears as a completely new piece. His rendition was entirely subjective and was also dependent on mood, yet was appropriate to the piece. On the other hand Liszt did not work for special virtuosic effects; he did not "show off" at the piano. Once when we talked about technique, in Rome in 1869, Liszt played for me his "Tristan" paraphrase, and I was fascinated; I no longer perceived any piano, and I believed that I was listening to Aeolus's harps.[88]

First surprise is registered by Draeseke's impression of the piece as rising like an improvisation. Second, he suggests the pianist's transformation of himself into firelike motion. Third, he notes that the pianist creates an original interpretation, but takes care not to deform the contents or "soul" of the composition. Finally, he highly valued Liszt's technique, which seemd to change the sound of the piano into another kind of instrument. Through the disinterested observations of Rappoldi and Draeseke on Liszt's technical and psychic/artistic faculties, the issue of the purely technical points of Liszt's performance will be examined.

LISZT'S PERFORMANCE: TECHNIQUE

Two German authors, C. A. Martienssen and O. V. Maeckl, writing their treatises on method in 1934 and 1938, respectively, make substantial mention of Liszt, both as a teacher and a performer. However, both authors selected situations which could justify similarities between their own methods of teaching and Liszt's; therefore, both render rather tendentious and misleading information, as in the case of Maeckl in *Das organische Klavierspiel,* Eiserhorn, 1938, who addresses the work of German writer C. F. Weitzmann (1808-1880).

This discussion starts with Weitzmann's controversial description of Liszt's hands on the piano in *Die Geschichte des Klavierspiels and Klavierliteratur.* Weitzmann asserts that Liszt was the founder of a revolution in modern piano playing, which is correct. However, on the position of Liszt's hands he makes a statement contrary to those writers quoted above; namely, that Liszt's wrist was considerably higher than was regarded proper in his time: "Finally, Liszt held the hand not horizontally, but with the wrist higher than the front part of the hand; so that if one were to put a penny on the back of the hand, the penny would be parallel with the keyboard."[89]

There is, in fact, pictorial evidence: many pictures, chiefly paintings, of Liszt sitting at instruments with his wrists raised. Why would these painters not paint a famous pianist accurately? Drawings, too, depict what this excerpt from the Preface of *Elementar-Klavierschule* by Karol Klindworth (1830–1916) tells us: "Characteristically Liszt changes the position of his hands often. In sections of those compositions whose content is of noble, pathetic, or elemental character his figure seems to grow. His shoulders and hands give the impression that he is spread out, over the keyboard. When executing light or lightning swift passages, his fingertips curl toward his palms, and he almost seems to be striking the keys with his nails."[90] The last sentence describes a position different from that described by Weitzmann; namely, the wrist held, not high; but still horizontal, parallel with the keys. Klindworth points out the curved position of the fingers.

Weitzmann's general view is one-sided. What could lead Weitzmann to this view, as static as the many painted depictions? A picture intentionally captures one moment, from many moments of a process, of the existence of a thing; but writing can place all of the elements in a process in juxtaposition, like the beads in a necklace. The hand position that Weitzmann describes would only occur at certain moments unavoidably, and be followed immediately by a relaxation of the hand. For anyone, much less Liszt, to perform in this position all of the time would be impossible, and contradictory to well-founded technique. As has been learned from the preceding descriptions of Liszt's technique, his positions of the hands and wrists depended upon the technique required by a given passage of music. Weitzmann's misapprehension can lead the uncritical or uneducated to adopt mannerisms of technique that are inappropriate and counterproductive.

Klindworth further writes on hand-position: "Liszt executed a soft, sweet, *cantabile* expression with dropped wrists, lower than the surface of the keyboard. It seemed that his stretched fingers, lightly lifted above the keys before attack, delicately pressed the keyboard."[91] There is no question of Klindworth's accuracy, as there is in the case of Weitzmann, whose observations were reproached by an army of professors in his own time. Imagine one professor teaching 15 students the technique of "high wrist." The possible consequences are far-reaching!

Liszt's famous student Hans von Bronsart raises an important principle of Lisztian technique, namely, the elasticity and total independence of all joints from one another, using his special term the "joint springs," working simultaneously as a perfect system of levers. This guarantees fine tone. This description by Bronsart, dated 1854, cannot be taken as a defense of Weitzmann's view. It is not known at which occasion this was mentioned; furthermore, it complicates the understanding of the following statement that "the hands must hover more in the air than stick upon the keys."[92] The expression "stick upon the keys" can point to placing the whole weight of the hands on the keys. "Hovering hands" are synonymous with elasticity manifested in the smooth lifting of the wrists, as they make contact with and depart from the keys.

Eyewitness descriptions are not ideal; they do not necessarily disclose reality, inasmuch as everyone perceives impressions uniquely, and everyone's memory is selective. A dozen people perceiving the same object will receive just as many separate impressions. Each person unconsciously gives an event his own individual coloration. By outlining several views here, an attempt has been made to derive more concrete knowledge, thus perhaps approaching the truth more closely. One view is limited to details of a motor nature (the "high wrist"), but the other views (Rappoldi, Schumann, Klindworth, *et al.*) help to give a fuller picture of Liszt as the outstanding Hungarian pianist.

6. German and French Treatises of the Nineteenth Century

Adolph Kullak: *Die Aesthetik des Klavierspiels*

In classifying and evaluating the theoretical and methodological works from the domain of pianistics in the nineteenth century, one is drawn immediately to the work of Adolph Kullak, in his *Die Aesthetik des Klavierspiels*. Kullak's work is the most extensive of all books on the subject of piano methods in the nineteenth century, in terms of the breadth of pianistic problems dealt with. Not only does it offer a broad synthesis of all the views of the nineteenth century; it also points into the twentieth, with its different stylistic issues.

The history of Kullak's 374-page book is not uninteresting: It was published ten times, first in 1861, and most recently in 1922, in Leipzig. During these 61 years, the publishers, Hans Bischoff and Walter Niemann, innovated and supplemented each edition, so that the last edition gives a complete picture of the so-called "Old Schools." The term "Old Schools" refers mainly to books on piano methods and piano manuals dating from the beginning of the nineteenth century, including the Classical and Romantic styles. The first edition of *Die Aesthetik* considered only the first half of the nineteenth century. The last edition in 1922 already includes the latent stage of the stylistic period, the early twentieth century. The latent stage of a new style is often a transitional period during which the views on a subject are exposed to severe or essential changes. The transitional period was captured by Kullak.

It is important to understand the stages of any new stylistic period or epoch in order to understand the difficult situation of Kullak's generation at the turn of the century. The music of Classicism was already dead, though it survived somewhat in the form of the Brahmsian symphony into the late nineteenth century. Late Romanticism reached its peak and then its decadent stage, in which the elements of the musical language had been overused or exaggerated, and the style could not develop further. The decadent stage of an epoch or stylistic period leads to overblown, sometimes inflated expression. The art loses its clearly defined, stylistic features, while the new features of the next epoch are emerging from their incipient, submerged stages to the surface. The new musical language, the new technique, and the new expressions appear for the first time, intermittently, and later more often, until at last they appear as a stabilized, explicit stage. When the epoch stabilizes, the elements of its musical language are again intensified; thus, the culmination appears; and then once again, decadence sets in.

The merit of Kullak lies in his undertaking the gigantic task of mapping the whole century, while other authors worked only in a limited continuum of time, without exploring the idea of universal knowledge. From this standpoint, Kullak's *Aesthetik* stands above his contemporaries' works. Kullak's work rests on the previous research of his predecessors, much like the music of Johann Sebastian Bach, whose work also synthesized all music created before him.

It is impossible to discuss here all of the knowledge that Kullak includes in his two parts of his book, containing eighteen chapters. The first part, to be brief, is entitled *Die Idee in allgemeinen,* and summarizes the entire evolution of the art of the piano. Excluded from consideration will be Kullak's views on the construction of instruments of the piano family, contained in the first chapter of the first part of his book.

The second chapter of the first part treats the history of keyboard virtuosity, which must be excluded from consideration. As a matter of sheer interest, I report the depth of his concern on the subject: He starts with the fifteenth- and sixteenth-century keyboard artists; that is, the German colorists, the English virginalists; continues with the early and late seventeenth- and eighteenth-century schools of the French, Italian and German clavecinists (Domenico Scarlatti, Johann Sebastian Bach and his sons); proceeds into the period of Classicism, including Haydn, Mozart, Clementi, Hummel, Moscheles, Cramer, Czerny, Dussek, and Beethoven; and follows the history through early Romanticism and then some more modern composers, such as Rubinstein, Schöenberg, and Edwin Fischer.

Kullak's third chapter is concerned with an historical review of keyboard methods, i.e., books and documents on piano performance. The development of actual practice in the twentieth century has ruthlessly refuted many of the "methods books" which had been celebrated in the past. Much of what is truthful theoretically has been verified with the passage of time, which became beneficial for our generation, and even the object of recent study. Kullak's positive contribution on the "methods books" concerns theoretical works from the beginning of the twentieth century. The results of new research in physiology, psychology, and acoustics of that time were applied to piano technique and musical perception, as well as techniques of musical memory. The new fields of piano methods were then opened to theorists. The merit of Kullak was that he was the first, at the end of the century, to introduce many unknown "methods books," which later became turning points in the history of piano methods. Such authors as Breithaupt, Steinhausen, Tetzel, Clark-Steininger, Matthay, Deppe-Caland, and Jaël initiated the psycho-physiological "current" of methods in the first decades of the twentieth century. L. Rieman initiated the acoustic-aesthetical "current." In full, these decades made artistic playing, technique, and the process of studying the pieces more conscious than it had been before, based upon logic of newly discovered movement of interpreters. All of the authors named above tried to free the process of interpretation from the "mechanics" of the study of music. They suggested "purposeful technique." However, these authors will not constitute the object of this investigation.

The core of this study's interest is the second part of Kullak's *Aesthetik*, entitled *Die Darstellung des Klavierschönen im besonderem*. Its principles of technique are described in eight chapters; the problems of interpretation, in seven chapters.

Before introducing Kullak's methodological thinking about the piano, it is necessary to critically evaluate the so-called "Old Schools" and the methods of the eighteenth century. The main characteristics to be proclaimed are empiricism and intuition, both constant sources of knowledge. This view had been broadened during the nineteenth century. The "Old Schools" do not take into account scientific argument. The problem thus starts at the basis of artistic performance; that is, in technique. Manuals of piano methods do not like to explain why certain ways or techniques are more progressive than others or more rational in their evolution. A typical characteristic is their emphasis on the external appearance of the moving apparatus or the player's arms and hands—not on the internal state of the interpreter.

Frédéric Chopin and Franz Liszt intuitively discovered the functions which direct the activity of our apparatus during piano playing. These functions later received various names and became the "Alpha and Omega" of the deliberations in books with a proclivity to the anatomic-physiological "current," as well as the psychological and physiological "currents" in the early twentieth century.

At the beginning of the twentieth century, there occurred the essential reversal in the evolution of piano technique. An entire *pléiade* of theoretical works had been published on the subject, having as a common denominator the intention to place this type of knowledge on a more scientifically solid basis. They also had in common the following features:

1) They infer that the material processes of interpretation derive from physics, more precisely, from mechanics; i.e., the weight and power of attack of the hand.

2) They emerge from what is empirical; i.e., the keen observation of the playing of famous pianists.

3) They deduce their inferences from the science of psychology, as for example in the case of the Hungarian author Margit Varrö in *Der lebendige Klavierunterricht*. The process of musical perception and memory was deliberated for the first time. Also, the sphere of the creative "will" was used as the main support for technique, as in *Die individuelle Klaviertechnik auf der Grundlage des schöpferischen Klangwillens* by Carl Adolph Martienssen.

4) The theory of F. Steinhausen takes up the critique of physiological mistakes in piano technique and of the faulty system of work, as well as the routine educational ways of the nineteenth century, often ignoring the naturalness of the movements, essentially the relaxation of the hand in the process of playing. The Steinhausen theory is interpreted in the book *Die physiologischen Fehler und Umgestaltung der Klaviertechnik*.

It is necessary now to return to Kullak's *Aesthetik* and the second critical drawback of the piano schools of the nineteenth century: The overused, one-sided treatment of finger technique. The methodologists mistakenly distinguished between technique and mechanics. They describe technique as explicitly oriented and consciously managed toward artistic and interpretational goals; mechanics, they believe, are gymnastic and unconscious. Kullak's writing does not dispute the existence of both, but he writes, "The mechanics ends where thinking begins. Technique begins when the mechanics have achieved a certain grade of perfection" (page 139). This view has been criticized by a famous student of Franz Liszt, who says that such a practice leads toward the situation in which "the person executing a piece no longer directs his playing, instead becoming a machine."[1]

The third characteristic of the "Old Schools," and with them Kullak also, is their failure to emphasize the varied movements of our moving apparatus, the forearm and the arm; and with such movements, the accompanying relaxation of the whole hand. Why? Because the main requirement of nineteenth-century books and treatises on methods, including Kullak's, was the use of small liftings of the fingers and slight movements in the processes of playing. Consequently, they used only the fingers and the wrists. With the coming of a new generation, as has been noted before, the situation changed so that the entire playing apparatus was set in motion, by revealing such new movements as flying, rotation, balancing, and circulative motion *(kreisbewegungen)*. Already Breithaupt and his followers had dispensed with the technique of small liftings, in his *Die natürliche Klaviertechnik*. The new motions totally revolutionized technique; on the other hand, they excluded finger technique absolutely, a small error because an entire historical development cannot be utterly cancelled. The technique of the fingers and the wrist was rehabilitated again somewhat later because certain technical formations, some effects, and certain extreme dynamic shadings of *pp* through *mp* directly require small movements with the upper parts of our moving apparatus, normally in a passive state. Kullak is extremely self-contradictory on this point. He introduces the statement (repeating the correct views of the outstanding theorists and teachers of the eighteenth and nineteenth centuries, Carl Phillip Emmanuel Bach, Marpurg, and Türk) that the position of the hand is changeable, depending on who is playing and what is being played, as long as the hand is free (Kulak, pages 140–151). Yet he is himself conservative, citing his opinion: "The chief requirement of all the positions and movements of the fingers is the tranquility of the hand...." (page 156).

Turning to a discussion of Kullak's positive and negative aspects, how is "Kullak's Theory" above average compared to other theories of the past? One must have certain reservations against his emphasizing the category of exercises entitled *Übungen mit gefesselter Hand* or *The Exercises with a Chained Hand*. With these exercises the education of the pianist begins. The *Exercises* represent the play of the fingers held motionless on the depressed keys, while the playing finger executes the attack. From the original: "...das heist alle Finger bleiben fest auf den heruntergedrückten Tasten stehen, während ein einziger sich im Anschlage übt" (page 156). Almost ten pages are devoted to a detailed description of the execution. The author does not agree with the extended immobility of the hand. She is in accord, rather, with the new view of the necessary harmonious cooperation of all parts of the hand during playing. Mention will now be made of Chopin's effort on the new fingering, in which each finger has its own individuality; this advantage can be utilized by the proper selection of the fingers, thus uprooting the theory of the "stillstehende Hand" (immobility of the hand).

The directive to hold the upper part of the body approximately 60 to

75 percent forward was obligatory in Kullak's time. In exceptional cases, such as that of Liszt, this requirement was not absolute. Augusta Boissier described the position of the upper part of the body as straight, with the head inclined slightly backwards.[2] One can rely on this description only partially, because Liszt could not have held his head slightly backwards all of the time; for instance, when he played passionate fragments. This can be evidence that Liszt intuitively loosened his playing apparatus during play.

The positive aspect of Kullak's book is still modern. He described five distinct positions of the hand which are still the starting point for various exercises:

1) when all fingers are held only on the white keys;

2) when the external fingers, the first and the fifth, are held upon white keys, while the middle finger or all other fingers are held on the black keys;

3) when one of the external fingers is held on a black key, and the remaining ones are held on white keys;

4) when the external fingers are both held on black keys, the middle finger or rest of the fingers remain on white keys;

5) when all of the fingers are held on the black keys.

The relation among distances can be changed five times. Each shift in position changes the task slightly. The most difficult position in Kullak's opinion is the fourth. In Chopin's view, the easiest position is the one of the hand in the E major scale (the first five fingers) because it is the most natural position, commensurate with the individual qualities of each finger. Chopin's natural position is equivalent to Kullak's second position. For the student of the present, the third position remains difficult in the same way.

In enumerating other positive features of Kullak's *Aesthetik,* the high precision and equalization of sound lines will first be introduced. This is the hallmark of all good methods of the nineteenth century. In order to achieve such a quality, entire generations, at least, must work on the power and independence of the fingers. In fact, the so-called *jeu perlé* or "pearly playing" is the result of elaboration carried to the point of perfection.

The sound revealing tenet of Kullak's thinking is his formation of the theory of the "singing attack," *Theorie des singenden Anschlag.* Throughout the nineteenth century, the view was held that legato playing could be based on a small, hammerlike attack or *hammerschlag.* The fingers were thought of as "knocking or clapping" on the keys. Kullak, however, rejected the attack produced this way. Instead of knocking and clicking into the keys, Kullak proposed his own requirement of the "singing" quality of the attack: "The finger must touch the key as if it were kneading or trying to make a fingerprint in wax, and the attack must be done with love and warmth" (page 236). In the "singing attack" the amplitude of finger movement has to be small, but the intensity of the finger's pressure on a piano key has to be forceful.

Pedaling is also a helpful agent in perfecting the execution of the singing or *cantilena*. The proper accompaniment to the singing tones of the *cantilena* must be in the background dynamically, unless the accompaniment contains notes of greater importance.

Kullak also deliberated about the "color effect" of tone. He found the use of "playing with higher lifting (of the fingers)" improper in quick passages, tremolos, and various types of trills. He suggests instead the opposite rule: "playing with lower lifting," literally, "Spiel mit niedrigen Aufheben" (page 236). This means that the fingers stay in the closest contact with the keyboard, thus adding a new color effect to the tones. Again literally from Kullak: "Sogar der Klavierton durch solche Behandlung seiner sinnlichen Klangmannigfaltigkeit wieder eine neue Farbe hinzufügt" (page 236).

Kullak is a modern author concerned with all the constituents of piano technique. He gives basic technical schemes which he abstracted from all possible technical situations in piano music. These represent the "keys/codes" for reading and finally mastering a given composition. The training material which Kullak presents is modern. It would be interesting to make a comparison between Liszt's elaborated "keys," mentioned in the previous chapter, and the following "keys" of Kullak:

1) five finger exercises in one position of the hand
2) octaves, broken octaves
3) sixths, fourths, thirds, etc.
4) diatonic and chromatic scales
5) passages
6) chords, broken chords
7) polyphonic exercises
8) shakes
9) repetitions, repetitive tones, intervals, chords, octaves
10) jumps
11) *glissando*

Today the keys and their variants are necessary for technique, but the operations performed with them are different from those of the nineteenth century. The mechanical material is not necessarily played as a daily quantity, but subordinated to the selection of the most convenient "keys," naturally changing the rhythm, the key signature, the dynamic shades, and the tone-color. Kullak's process is more creative than that of his predecessors.

The second part of Kullak's *Aesthetik,* "Der Vortrag" or "Interpretation," passes on to one of the most interesting questions in art, to the creation of what is beautiful music. The aesthetic interpretation begins with the details of musical language, such as precise comprehension of rhythm and accents. The choice and location of accents, main and secondary, require not only intuition, but reason. The accents occur in a measure as a small unit, but also on a larger scale, in a phrase. Accents have a certain hierarchy, which still causes problems and faulty interpretations. Some examples from Kullak are presented, which represent the most prevalent mistakes in both the preceding and present centuries, despite the evolution of methods. (All examples are from Kullak, pages 296–297.)

The fugue theme below by J. S. Bach has the main accent on "G," as marked in the second measure. The accent on "G" is for the sake of syncopation:

Similar reasons determine the accent on the following theme, in the C Minor Fugue:

The following theme has the metric, measure accent on F sharp:

The same applies in the theme (secondary) of Beethoven's Sonata in C Major, Op. 53. The main accent is on the first beat, in the second and fourth measures; the secondary accent is on the first beat, in the first and third measures. The G sharp in the last measure demands a slightly greater weight.

The following example is from Scriabin's Sonata No. 4, in the Second Movement. The accent is placed not on the highest note, D-sharp, in the first measure; but on the A-sharp in the second measure, as a strong metric accent, and the longest rhythmic value (note):

The following theme needs the accent (emphasis) on the two G's on account of the length and pitch proportion. Beethoven's Sonata in C Major, Op. 53, or "Waldstein Sonata," in the Third Movement:

The accentuation in the next three measures is decided by the pitch relation, although all of the tones must be played singingly. Beethoven, Sonata in G Major, Op. 14:

Similarly the highest A, in the second measure, has the strongest accent. The F-sharp, as a part of the chord, in the third measure, has a milder accent, essentially because of the chord length and the descending character of the fourth and fifth measures of the example. (All examples below are from Kullak, pages 302–303.)

The Allegro by Carl Maria von Weber, from his F Minor Concerto, has three accents: the first because of the tone-pitch; both others, on metric grounds.

The last example selected is from Henselt's F Minor Concerto for Piano and Orchestra, in the First Movement. The accents are for reasons of both metrics and tonality.

After the problems of accentuation, the next issue in the hierarchy is Kullak's observation of the measure or bar. The counterbalance of the beat in a measure is one of the most important issues in the art of music. The music of Classicism and the Baroque are especially constructed upon metric regularity and vibrant pulsation, similar to the biological rhythms of the human body, and on orderly playing. Metric "order" depends on exact rhythm and art to maintain the beat. This requires, as mentioned before, correct accentuation of the notes or the rhythms into the larger units.

The "Old Schools" put great emphasis on the importance of the measure. Kullak takes up the equivalent viewpoint. He could not predict the forthcoming changes; they came with the appearance of Impressionism and "Twelve-Tone Technique" of the Viennese School at the beginning of the twentieth century. He expresses the typical view: "Der Takt sei die Seele der Musik"—"The measure is the soul of the music" (page 271). Analyzing this statement, one can form a counter-statement. If the measure is really the "soul" of the music, then the music is monotonous. The "soul" of the music is created by all of the constituents of expression and technique in equilibrium. In fact, some concrete programmatic compositions depend solely on "the measure" in order to create a musical picture of a machine or of regular processes as in marches, toccatas, etc., as in the compositions of Prokofiev, Pasquini, and Honneger. The contradiction comes when the requirement of irregularity in music is introduced; for instance, the tempo rubato, as was used already by Mozart in the eighteenth century, and continuing, for example, with Chopin's compositional techniques. The cadences in concertos for a solo instrument with the orchestra, such as in the music of Scriabin, Liszt, and Brahms, require the violation of metrical regularity in some places as a rule. Liszt's famous statement, quoted in Augusta Boissier's *Liszt als Lehrer,* makes the same claim: "...seien Sie nicht so im Takt," meaning, "Do not emphasize the measure so much." As Milstein's fragment confirms: "I would like to make an end of the mechanical interpretation, which is broken into the bars, as far as possible."[3] Liszt warns us to understand his music within the frame of small cells or measures. Thus Liszt's pieces are played only as a mathematical juxtaposition of equal beats of time.

The tendentious views of present pedagogics have too long prevailed. The meticulous holding on to the rhythm, in the sense of time-values, and the bar, exerted such a strong influence on the whole interpretation that the critics of that time often did not understand the statements of Chopin or Liszt. Huneker's *Chopin* offers many examples of the misunderstanding of Chopin's rubato. Even Berlioz and other critics complained that Chopin did not play in a strict measure!

The next issue to be discussed are the thoughts of Kullak on rhythm. Excerpted here is a mysterious proposition of Hans von Bülow from Kullak's chapter on rhythm in order to illustrate what dominates all other thoughts introduced by Kullak: "Im Anfang war der Rythmus," translating to, "At the beginning was rhythm" (page 271). The "Alpha and Omega" of musical understanding is rhythm; at the beginning of the matter itself was the rhythm of sound, that is, the physical-acoustical phenomenon. The radio-electrical signals of Venus, Mars, and Pluto have been interpreted as certain sounds of low, higher, and very high frequency, with various pulsations of rhythmical qualities. Kullak's generation did not have the information from the universe that we now have; therefore, the citation from Kullak has an even more mysterious significance.

Also from Kullak: "In counting aloud while practicing music, all will sound equal, distinctive, and round; and the interpreter will gain more assurance in performing the piece, than if he does not count aloud" (page 271). In our century this view cannot be accepted, because counting aloud instead becomes an operation of our consciousness. We perceive by our "inner ear," mentally, without pronounced counting. In this manner we can hear the pure sound of music. Counting interferes with the sound and disturbs the attention to music as it is being played. Excepting this, Kullak's book cannot be negated, and the chapter on rhythm cannot be discounted. Positive examples can be found in Kullak's book, but not revealing ones. The point is to know how to use them correctly.

Summarizing Kullak's contribution to our generation, one should speak about other issues, also important parts of the interpretative musical art, such as accelerando, rallentando, dynamics, phrasing, pedaling, tone-coloration, and finally, aesthetic issues, such as the musical idea, the concept of the work as art, as well as musical integrity and style. It is regrettable that Kullak utterly omitted relevant discussions on phrasing, fingering, styles, and musical memory. But fortunately he did not omit the remaining parts of the interpretative art: agogics, dynamics, and pedaling. It would be repetitive to discuss them, however, since he does not reveal any new ideas.

In Kullak's time, processes such as the learning of musical pieces by memorization of musical texts had not yet been investigated and not yet been linked with the general laws of psychology and physiology. The schools had compiled hours and hours of mechanical training until the stage of completion. The present gaps in this part of *Die Aesthetik* are not a result of Kullak's disinterest, but the level of methods achieved at that time. The same situation was reflected in violin schools, as a parallel example. Kullak speaks here only for the views of his own epoch. Time is merciless, testing all theories and refuting them; however, Kullak's theories were not totally uprooted by the epoch that followed.

Closing remarks will be devoted to the supreme aesthetic meditation of Kullak—primarily, to his beliefs concerning integration of the musical piece as a whole. Only in the last pages of the book does he place a tiny section, which narrates in the philosophic sense how a work of art is created from the details, which are aimed toward an integrated musical piece, which is to be interpreted in the process of time. Kullak's whole book explains music, in both its details and its parts. The synthesis of art is to find proportions among the fragments and to submit them to a unifying, holistic idea, which is often expressed in the title of a musical piece. All of the extremes must be rounded into a finished work. Kullak himself says so much. No one detail can protrude into the foreground. Certain parts are subordinated to higher parts and are again arranged in a particular order, organically bonded to one another. They form a pyramid, with the "Platonic idea" dominating the top of the triangular form. From the top, the most important part, the lower levels are deducible. Conversely, all levels connect at the top level, completing the thought. Such an ideal shape is architectonically indestructible, geometrically forming a perfectly counterbalanced shape. The musical ideas must shine as the primordial source.

With regard to this concept, Kullak's book thoroughly discusses a multitude of particularities. Kullak states the wish that elaboration of details would not absorb the entire attention of the player or student. Such a situation often occurred in the nineteenth century as a "love for polishing details." The theorem about the integration of the whole and dialectical processes was not obvious in Kullak's theories. The ideal of the "Old Schools" is valued and appreciated, as well as Kullak's theories; namely, the systematically cultivated idea of the order, harmony, and clarity of each melodic line were contributions which have expanded musical horizons. Kullak's hints, instructions, and precepts, as dispersed among approximately the last hundred pages of his *Aesthetik,* aim toward this ideal. At the beginning of the twentieth century, this ideal dissolved and has been replaced since then by an expressionistic style of interpretation. Now, however, Kullak's contribution has once again been rehabilitated. The greater portion of Kullak's last chapter as well as his book as a whole have certainly retained their value today.

Mathis Lussy: *Traité de l'expression musicale*

For the concert pianist, the last and most important treatise of the nineteenth century is by the well-known French music theorist Mathis Lussy, and is entitled *Traité de l'expression musicale.* Published in Paris in 1873, it immediately became the most respected and recommended discussion on its subject.

The essay's distinction is that it was written, not only for pianists and other keyboardists, but also for orchestral directors, vocalists, and other instrumentalists. Although published more than a century ago, the book still has something to tell us — particularly those of us who study the rules of execution prescribed for all nineteenth-century musicians. In addition Lussy's essay is recommended to music theorists as well, and even to music critics, who will gain insight into the mystery of the interpreter's art.

The discussion was originally dedicated to Monsieur F. A. Gevaert, master of the Belgian King's Chapel and director of the Royal Conservatory in Brussels; but its importance lies in its dedication to musical art and to the laws of musical expression. In the nineteenth century, the term "expression" was used to describe the highest interpretive artistry. Romanticism has intensified musical expression, a development which may be observed by surveying what preceded it, during the late period of the Renaissance; the Baroque, with its theory of affects; then early and late Classicism. As one century followed another, rules and principles proliferated, giving rise to the impulse for order and classification. The French public had long awaited a treatment of musical expression topically, and Lussy's book provided it.

Lussy's *Traité* has been translated into English, German, and Russian. But in other European countries and in the United States, the treatise is still practically unknown. For this reason, a considerable amount of space will be devoted to its discussion. Lussy's book presents numerous maxims and propositions on the aesthetic and stylistic interpretation of music, as well as uncountable practical examples from vocal, instrumental, and keyboard music. According to Lussy, both theoretical rules and practical examples should be used in musical education for the purpose of developing artistic or "expressive" execution. Lussy's examples range from the simplest romances to works of transcendent artistic importance. Some of Lussy's conclusions are common knowledge today; others have become obsolete. Conclusions falling into either category are omitted from the presented discussion.

In Lussy's time, much effort had been devoted to marking the interpretive signs which denote dynamics, tempo changes, and accentuation. Most of this work had been done on the masterworks of vocal and keyboard music. The effort, though great, was not sufficient, because of changes in the social role of music in the latter half of the nineteenth century. Rather than a field for professionals with special training and talent, music became more and more accessible to the general public. The situation led to a growing dichotomy between musicians of only mediocre talent and technique, and musicians who gave to their interpretation a level of sophisticated, deliberate expression. Lussy tried to reconcile this dichotomy in his essay. He writes in the Preface: "Only musical expression is the soul of music, and this remains the exceptional quality of some individuals with an inborn talent" (page 2). The social conditions of Lussy's era allowed all people to be involved with music, but "not all are equally talented" (page 2).

On the other hand, pedagogues cannot annotate all musical literature in detail, and even if they could, interpreters would not understand the reasons for the markings. Signs and symbols denote precisely where it is necessary to accentuate, to accelerate, to slow down, etc.; but they do not explain why to play in one manner and not in another. The point is to know thoroughly what leads one to choose between forté and piano, between rallentando and accelerando, and so on. In a really artistic execution, no one note can be arbitrarily accentuated.

In his essay, Lussy aims first of all to introduce the rational assumptions, unknown until his book appeared, which would guide artists and professors in the problems of interpretation; and second, to furnish rules enabling all interpreters to independently mark each musical composition, enabling virtually all performers to play all sorts of music with expression, whether scored for vocal, keyboard, or instrumental performance.

Lussy prefaces his treatise with a disclaimer to the effect that he did not originate the rules that he presents. The greatest masters, such as Chopin and Liszt, observed and used these rules continually, though unconsciously, as did those of cultivated taste, prior to Lussy's treatise. But Lussy was the first to uncover and to formulate the principles of musical expression, especially the phenomenon of accentuation. On this subject, Lussy is the only nineteenth-century theorist who researched and compiled all possibilities, and then attempted to classify them and to determine the common factors among various groups. On other phenomena of musical expression, such as dynamics, Lussy's treatment is interesting but not innovative. The same may be said of his discussions of tempo in his chapter about "contrasting movements," as well as the graduation of musical phrases and motives. The graduation is one of the final elements of a smooth transition between the contrasting sections of crescendo and decrescendo.

The most important feature of Lussy's essay is its attempt to limit individual empiricism, by placing the questions raised by interpretation in the domain of the intellect. The essay also fills a gap in musical pedagogy and theory, existing since the time of the late French Baroque clavecinists, of the treatise *La Traité de mélodie* by Antonín Rejcha.

In this section attention will be focused on Lussy's most illuminating ideas on artistic interpretation, i.e., those concerning accentuation, inasmuch as musical expression cannot exist without this precept. Lussy classifies accentuation under three headings: metrical accents, rhythmic accents, and pathetic accents. How does one perceive each in the process of listening?

Lussy describes metrical accents as strong accents, evoking mild movement of the listener's head or leg, and clearly indicating the measure. The listener reacts to the metrical accents instinctively. "When we listen to the piece, as the melody ascends and descends, some sounds seem to be stronger; others, weaker. The strong pulses occur at regular intervals, separating each measure from the next by their repeated accentuation" (page 2). Metrical accents, Lussy notes, are easily detectable in marching or in the action of an oarsman or a blacksmith.

The musical literature, carefully observed and classified by Lussy in his Chapter 5 on metrical accentuation, enabled him to generate rules for ideal interpretative achievement. It is necessary to state that these rules are not illuminating and do not answer all of the questions which are important for interpretation. Impressionism and Modern music made Lussy's rules obsolete. In spite of this, a couple of examples of metrical accents, typical of the problems of Lussy's epoch, will be introduced, restating once more how often pedagogues make it clear that metrical accents can be felt, yet still students struggle with this old problem of accentuation. The examples are excerpted from Lussy's *Traité* on pages 73, 76, and 78.

Rossini. *Stabat*.

Auber. *Haydée*.

The stronger the rhythmic value of the note, particularly if it is the first note in a measure, the more the note is accented.

The following example illustrates the simple four-beat measure with notes on the first and third beats accented, the main and secondary accents, and with the notes on the second and fourth beats having no metrical accents:

Rhythmic accents are not so easily detectable as metrical accents are. They are, however, strong; moreover, Lussy describes them as being to music what punctuation is to speech. Rhythmic accents exact a certain effort of the intellect. Rhythmic accents, then, punctuate musical phrases in all of their constituent elements, appearing either symmetrically or asymmetrically. Rhythmic accents are not identical with metrical accents and are in fact sometimes placed against them.

The examples from vocal literature which Lussy uses demonstrate that the beginnings of verses or half-verses often converge with the rhythmic accents. Generally, one can say that the rhythmic accents demarcate individual tone groups which possess musical ideas.

It is in the process of listening to music that one perceives most clearly the independence of the metrical and rhythmical systems because they can actually be heard playing, as if pitted against one another. The examples cited below will make this distinction even clearer.

The next example will introduce the problem of rhythmic accents. A measure in 3/4 time has by definition one metrical accent, on the first beat. Often, however, the third beat in a measure is meant to be lightly accented; see examples a, b, and c, where the accents placed on the last beat are created by dividing the second note into two smaller rhythmical values. The examples cited are from Grisar, Chopin, and Weber, respectively.

a) Grisar.

b) Chopin.

c) Weber.

Example a is a second instance of rhythmic accentuation, on the third beat of the example given; on the last note of the phrase, the arsis, which may cause an objection. As the rules in common cases affirm, the last note of the phrase should be dynamically the softest. Why is the case an exception to the common rule? Lussy finds the reason: The last note is preceded by a pause (as in example below). Example below shows a motive without a pause, therefore the end of the motive is not accentuated.

a)

b)

The example from Lussy's page 77, illustrated by Beethoven's famous "Mondschein Sonata" or "Moonlight Sonata," Op. 27, elucidates another important rule of Lussy's: "The note which falls on or underneath a prolongation, or on a silence, or under a silence at the beginning of a measure, must be accented," as follows in both of the examples below (page 102):

On the topic of pathetic or emotional accents, Lussy is at his most original and illuminating. At the time, "pathetic" meant simply "emotional," and Lussy's original usage will be maintained. Pathetic accents are independent of the two types of accents described above. They manifest themselves unexpectedly, interrupting the musical flow, disturbing the order and regularity of the measure and of the existing rhythm. The examples from Lussy's book demonstrate how these accents often change the whole mood of the surrounding passage. As Lussy says: "This type of accent is perceived primarily through the ability called musicality; . . .

these accents startle one emotionally...." (page 3). (See the examples below.)

Lussy's conclusions are interesting; his hierarchy of ideas, well formulated. Although the measure is one of the basic elements of music, for Lussy the metrical accents are those lowest in the hierarchy. Next in importance are the rhythmic accents; but the pathetic accents are supreme. By giving greatest emphasis to the emotional element, Lussy unconsciously links himself to the next stylistic period in the history of music, Impressionism.

Some examples will now be introduced from Lussy's extensive Chapter 6, entitled "On Pathetic Accentuation" (page 96). The fragment from Meyerbeer illustrates Lussy's rule on how to recognize pathetic accents. When a measure is situated in a musical passage composed of sounds with varying rhythmic values, in which one sound falls within each unit; whether it be an interval, a chord, or even just one note; and there are several; and they all ascend; then each sound must be accented.

Meyerbeer

The asterisks indicate the pathetic accents.

The following three examples again refer to pathetic accents. In this case Lussy gives another rule, which he put in a modern way: The more a given sound seems to interfere with the sound anticipated, the more strongly the interrupting sound must be accented. The interrupting sound can be a dissonance, an alteration, a delay, or an alternating note.

a) Mozart: Delay
b) Rossini: Dissonance
c) Beethoven: Alteration

More explanation of the alternating note, also called the upper note, is needed. This is the most common case of pathetic accentuation. The alternating (upper) sound is extremely emotional and requires an emphasis. This emphasis is extremely important in the following circumstances:

1) when it initiates the rhythmic figure;
2) when its rhythmical value is greater than the other values in a given context;
3) when it is the penultimate or next to last sound in a rhythmical figure; and
4) when it occurs after the pause.

The examples are taken from Chopin, Gounod, Rossini, and Verdi, as follows:

1)

CHOPIN. Op. 9, n° 3. *Nocturne.*

2)

GOUNOD. *Faust.*

3)

ROSSINI. *Barbier.*

4)

VERDI. *Le Trouvère.*

If a survey is critically made from Lussy's comments and ideas on accentuation, one can at least summarize his 40 examples and nine rules: The more obviously a note follows from the preceding ones, the less forceful its accentuation needs to be. The opposite also follows: The more a note is distorted—that is, the more it seems to be an obstacle to an expected note—the more important its accentuation. The interruption can be in the form of repetitive notes, a dissonant note or chord, a delayed note, a chromatic note, a note of extended rhythmical value, etc. Such a note requires a more forceful accentuation. This is in reality the pathetic accent described by Lussy. One might say our ear perceives the interruptions as violence; just as in Baroque architecture where the middle part of a façade of a palace protrudes so dynamically, interruptions seem to violate harmony.

The last and most eloquent example, in summation of all which has come before, is from Beethoven's "Sonata Pathétique," the Second Movement: The more grandiose and enharmonic the modulations, the greater value of the note compared to the surrounding notes; hence the repetitiveness, the main and secondary accents, the metrical accents, all are immediately apparent:

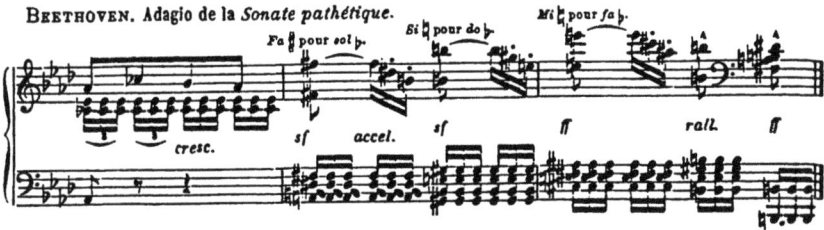

Lussy assumes, as he writes in the Preface, on page three, that a couple of months would be sufficient in order to acquaint all musicians with the reasons for accents and the other subtleties of dynamics and tone intensity. Today it is believed that a thorough knowledge of this extensive field of musical interpretation would require several years of study, because musical literature is not composed of various examples of categorized patterns, but rather of an infinite variety of unique cases.

Since musical interpretation consists of the relationship between kinetic, dynamic, and static movements, it cannot focus only upon accentuation. There are essential fusing elements, like tempo changes and various shadings of tonal intensity. It is the gradation of a musical phrase which gives ultimate meaning to the more mechanical elements. The question of how to achieve this gradation is a complex and nuanced one, and therefore requires further discussion. Lussy tries to encompass all possible categories of tempo changes, which he terms "emotional" changes.

The three types of alteration in tempo are accelerando, rallentando, and tempo rubato. Tempo rubato is not dealt with in Lussy's system, nor are phrasing and pedaling.

The accelerando results from the animation of the artist and his effort to render pathetic accents, which ascend one after another. The accelerando results furthermore from monotonous sound structure, from the fatigue or exhaustion which follows an emotional passage (in Lussy's description, "les fragments passionnés"), from the presence of an unpredictable obstacle, or from a complicated emotional context. All of these things cause "emotional" alterations in tempo. In order to fully substantiate such a multifarious phenomenon as accelerando, one should consider some of Lussy's examples. These examples and similar ones continue even today to cause problems in playing the Classical and Romantic literatures of the piano.

"[When] the note ... has in its context quite extensive rhythmic value or when the note is a syncope, and it is accompanied by a base of ascending or descending tendency, then there is an *accelerando*" (Lussy, page 119). Lussy, in fact, uses the term "excitement" for accelerando.

V. MASSÉ. *Noces de Jeannette*.

In the case of Mozart's Fantasia in D Minor, the bass tends to descend to repeat the "D," as follows:

It is valuable to know another of Lussy's rules, concerning a group of notes which are repeated exceptionally, if the bass ascends or descends (Lussy, page 120). The example shows the descending bass:

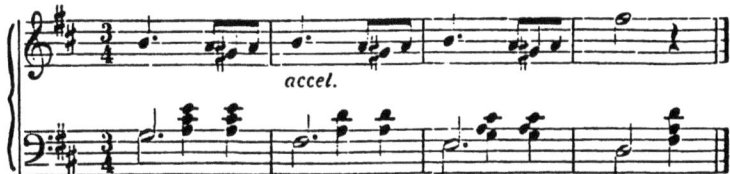

The accelerando is also determined by harmonic modulation, especially at the beginning or at the end of a motive. Lussy refers to the motive as a "rhythm," which causes confusion in his text. The example is from Beethoven's "Sonata Pathétique" in C Minor (Lussy, page 121):

The third measure is complex, since it contains not only the modulation on the dominant, but also an ascending melody in the right hand, the descending movement of the accompaniment, and the countermovement between the melody and the accompaniment.

All of the cases possible cannot be considered here. After careful deliberation, the following examples have been chosen in order to introduce the most necessary solutions.

The following three rules deal with interruption of the musical continuum. Freely interpreted from Lussy: If the phrase or passage is interrupted by a pause and simultaneously syncopated (on the theses), then there is an accelerando.

Più mosso, in both of the examples from Mozart, indicates an accelerando:

MOZART. *Fantaisie en ré mineur.*

MOZART. *Sonate en fa.*

The following rule will apply: In cases where the phrases or passages are exceptionally syncopated, an accelerando is needed.

BEETHOVEN. Op. 26.

The phrase that is accompanied by chords, coming after the preceding phrase with broken chords, must be accelerated. The example of the Nocturne by Field shows quiet, stationary chords with regular structure, as follows:

FIELD. 5ᵉ *Nocturne.*

The bass is decisive for accelerando, even in cases where the bass remains stationary, and a small group of notes is repeated more than once. This occurs at the end of a section with a vivid, agile tempo. Beethoven's Sonata in C-sharp Minor, "The Moonlight Sonata," can serve as a classic example.

A similar situation occurs in Mozart's Sonata in A Major, in the Minuet:

The following sentence can be added to Lussy's analysis of accelerando: The accelerando is self-evident in passages which are situated in a passionate or agitated context, as in Beethoven's "Sonata Pathétique":

Lussy is a paradigmatical theorist, as to the next and opposite constituent of musical expression, the rallentando. Therefore, one should attempt to learn more about his work on this subject, even if only to gain a brief impression of a complex, if scattered, system. From Lussy's next to last chapter, only a few rules will be presented, although this chapter offers an encyclopedic array of examples and explanations, mainly from Lussy's own epoch (though he does not forget to mention the masters of the sixteenth and seventeenth centuries). This brief selection is in no way intended to minimize Lussy's effort.

Many of us today often hear incomplete interpretations on the artistic stage, rendered by important artists. Why? These artists do not read ancient essays; nor do they carefully take the time to gather knowledge of the theorists, composers, interpreters, or famous pedagogues through the centuries, who have conserved the precious statements and observations on the understanding and interpretation of music. In order to stop the continual errors in present-day interpretations, rules collected and systematized by Lussy are introduced here. Unconsciously played fragments can be illustrated by the following examples:

1) The rallentando results from the end of an ascending or descending process, from the exhaustion of strengths or from enthusiasm. These two examples are from mazurkas by Chopin (Lussy, page 128):

Chopin. Op. 30, 2.

Chopin. Op. 7, 2°.

2) The rallentando results from the ascending melodic line with the notes of the highest pitch; if they are followed by a low note, they create a considerable leap. Before the second note is a rallentando, in the Beethoven example before B-flat, in the next to last measure; the same in the first Mozart example, before the C note; and in the next Mozart example, before the A tone, with a turn sign (Lussy, page 128):

3) A rallentando comes at the syncopated, prolonged, or chromatic note, when placed at the end of the last measure (Lussy, page 132):

4) A rallentando occurs at a note repeated several times, immediately (Lussy, page 132):

5) A rallentando in expressive passages provokes a rêverie, inserted in the middle of a particularly vivid phrase (Lussy, page 130):

The vocal literature has many principles in common with instrumental music, which may be seen here in the following examples, which are from Lussy, page 127:
1) A rallentando is made at a high-pitched note, if the note represents the counterpart of the low note.

AUBER. *Haydée.*

2) A rallentando occurs when ascending groups are immediately followed by descending groups. Four measures are needed to order to ascend and two measures are required for the counterbalance, by making the rallentando, in the Bellini example below. In the Gounod example, the ratio is 5:3, so that the rallentando is done upon the smaller area in the last three measures:

Bellini. *Norma.*

GOUNOD. *Faust.*

3) One makes a rallentando at a long note which precedes the final note, and especially when the long note is to be trilled. This principle is easily illustrated; the example is from instrumental music, an ancient air:

Air ancien.

4) In music, mainly in the epochs of Classicism and Romanticism, the law of contrast between major and minor measures appears often in both vocal and instrumental music. When the minor measure appears after the major, it is necessary to make a rallentando. The Rossini, Beethoven, and Mozart examples move from the major tonality in the fourth measure (Rossini), the first measure (Beethoven), and the first

measure (Mozart), to the minor in the eighth measure (Rossini), the second measure (Beethoven), and the third measure (Mozart). All three examples are presented from Lussy, even though they are well known. It is well worth noting that major-minor phenomena are most frequent at the end of soft expressive phrases. Even mediocre interpreters execute this musical structure instinctively, because the reason for it is obvious: The final note is the pivot-point of the musical phrase. Or, differently stated, all "attractions" in Classicism come at the end:

This fourth point has been expanded more than the previous three in order to accustom the interpreter to a detailed analysis, and also to attract his attention to the multiple aspects of such phenomena as rallentando and accelerando.

Next, a few examples will be provided which help to explain Lussy's section on musical dynamics, entitled *Des nuances et de l'intensité de son*. The effect of the metrical, rhythmical, and pathetic accents produces contrasts or forcefulness. Each accented note weakens its neighboring notes, just as light and shade exist together. The accents alone are not able to make the music poetic or dramatic. The contrasts may very well sound abrupt and jerky. The passages must be connected by gradations, measured tastefully, delicately, even softly. Transitions made this way will fuse the contrasts into harmonious unity.

Each composition, indeed each phrase, has its own intensity of sound—the sonority—commensurate with its context. The task of the interpreter is to grade the dynamics of the piece independently. Gradually increasing sonority, the crescendo, whether in a small motive or in voluminously long pieces, is employed in ascending lines. This vocal example is from Lussy, page 139, excerpted from Rossini's "Stabat Mater":

The gradation in this example seems pitted against "obstacles," the gradually ascending passage with dotted rhythm.
The decrescendo is employed in descending lines. The passage loses vehemence and sonority in the last four measures of this example from Beethoven and in the last four measures of the example from Chopin (Lussy, page 139). The end of both decrescendos is played gently, without intensity, as follows:

BEETHOVEN. *Le Délire du cœur.*

Cœur ardent, cœur en dé - li-re, Et dé - faillant tour à tour, Ah! fais trêve à ton mar-ty-re, En l'oubliant un seul jour.

CHOPIN. Op. 55.

The exception to this rule is Lussy's rule of modulation, when one must make a crescendo in spite of the descending tendency of the line. This happens when the descending passage contains the modulation, or the immediately unforseen obstacles, or the "pathetic" notes (Lussy, page 193):

The important ideas of the *Traité de l'expression musicale* have been presented sufficiently. A longer passage from Lussy is now quoted in order to give the reader the flavor of his original language, and to get him acquainted with the suggestions for pedagogues, which best illustrate Lussy's intentions:

> Each pedagogue should direct the student's attention toward the construction of phrases in the musical piece, toward the changes of melody and harmony, toward the tonal, metrical, and rhythmical irregularities, so to say, upon all of the exceptional, unforeseen sounds, which compel expressiveness and exact from the listener accustomed to observing, comparing, and analyzing musical phenomena. Who knows? Maybe then the pedagogue will be persuaded that his students possess not only perception, but also culture, knowledge, mental discipline,

and the faculty to manifest their impressions to the audience. The students undoubtedly gain independence when they know the elements of expression in music and learn to perceive, in the renditions of great artists, the tools of musical expression, serving to create human emotions and experiences. In consequence of such a relationship to music, students will cease to follow their pedagogues blindly and will try by themselves to find the secret of interpretative art. Consequently their playing becomes living, vital, emotional, and full of poetry (page 9).

The presentation of Lussy's views concludes with a final criticism, concerning the weakness common to all his diverse theoretical instructions in the field of dynamics, tempi, agogics, and accentuation. In the entire essay, he makes no mention of the strength of a particular accent, the grade of a given crescendo or dimenuendo; i.e., the note at which the given fragment of the piece should be slowed down or accelerated. Here it must be stated that theory and knowledge can create an elaborate interpretive scheme for a given work of art; but at the moment when this scheme is transformed into real sounds, the decisive factor is the aural imagination of the interpreter. Only the interpreter can determine the grade of tension and timbre of the sound, as well as the tempo of the piece.

As has been said before, Lussy's book does not discuss such important elements of interpretation as phrasing (connection or disconnection between musical phrases and small motives) and pedaling (connection and disconnection of sounds and chords by use of the pedal). Nor does Lussy attempt to explain what this study has tried to convey by the term "ear," the aural imagination that makes excellent interpretation possible. This problem remains to challenge those interested in interpretation, and will continue to intrigue artists, theorists, and pedagogues well into the next century.

Appendix: The Tablet of the Development of the Elements

	Couperin	*J. Bach*	*C. Bach*	*Türk*	*Mozart*
Posture at the Piano	/				↑
Hand Position	/	↑			↑
Finger Position			/		↑
Finger Fixation			/		
Shape of the Palm			/		
Touch	/	↑			
Muscular Relaxation	/		↑		
Motor Response or Hand Mechanics			/	↑	
Tone	/	↑		↑	↑
Dynamics			/	↑	
Rhythm				/	↑
Agogics	/			↑	↑
Phrasing				/	
Articulation	/	↑		S	
Plasticity of the Playing			/	S	
Ornaments	↑	↑	S		
Fingering	/	↑		↑	S
Pedalling					
Registration					
Methological Process	/	↑	↑	↑	

The undiscovered fields in the piano methods have a blank column.
The first appearance or the first discovery of the element has the sign /.
The complement or extension of the element is marked by ↑.
The systemization of the element/problem has the sign S.

Notes

1. Predecessors of the Piano

1. A. Modr, *Hudební nástroje* (Musical Instruments), Prague, 1977, page 71.
2. W. Chmielowska, *Z zagadnień nauczania gry na fortepiane* (From Questions of Learning to Play the Piano), Kraków, 1963, page 11.
3. Z. Böhmová, *Kapitoly z dějin klavírních škol* (Chapters in the History of Keyboard Schools), Prague, 1973, page 11.
4. Henricus Arnaut von Zwolle's description in his treatise from Bohdan Pociej, *Klavesyniści francuscy*, Polskie Wydawnictwo muzyczne, Kraków, 1969.
5. Chmielowska, *op. cit.*, page 13. See also A. Modr, *op. cit.*, page 72.
6. A. Modr, *op. cit.*, page 72.

2. French Methods of the Seventeenth and Eighteenth Centuries

1. See *The First Book of Toccatas* by G. Frescobaldi, published in Rome in 1637 during the composer's lifetime. The original title reads: *Toccate D'Intavolatura di Cimbalo et Organo*.
2. François Couperin, *L'Art de toucher...*, page 9.
3. *Ibid.*, page 10.
4. *Ibid.*, page 11.
5. *Ibid.*, page 13.
6. *Ibid.*, page 11.
7. *Ibid.*
8. *Ibid.*, pages 10, 11, 13.
9. *Ibid.*, pages 11, 12.
10. *Ibid.*, page 12.
11. In original (Couperin, page 16) is written: "Manière pour lier plusieurs pincés...." ("How to bind several consecutive mordents").
12. Couperin, *op. cit.*, pages 19, 20.
13. *Ibid.*, page 18.
14. *Ibid.*
15. François Couperin, *The Art of Playing the Harpsichord*, fascimile, Alfred Publishing Company, 1974, page 39.
16. Although the new numbering of the fingers appeared earlier in Girolamo Diruta's treatise *Il transilvano* in Venice, 1593, nevertheless almost all tasks in playing

have been entrusted to three middle fingers. Other examples can be seen in the English virginal music literature of high renaissance era, in Sweelinck's case, etc.

17. Couperin, *L'Art de toucher...*, page 17.
18. *Ibid.*
19. *Ibid.* pages 12, 17.
20. Couperin writes exactly: "The repercussion ... must all be included in the value of the principal note." *L'Art de toucher...*, page 15.
21. *Ibid.*, pages 17, 37 (5-14 measures), 38 (measures 4, 9, 18), 39 (measures 1-3, 5-10, 16, 23, 24).
22. *Ibid.*, page 17.
23. Today's "slide" is fully written out in a form of two consecutive notes of equal values, usually ascending or descending before the main note. There is no dotted rhythm.
24. Couperin, *The Art of Playing the Harpsichord*, facsimile, Alfred Publishing Company, 1974, page 73.
25. *Ibid.*, page 15.
26. François Couperin, *Complete Keyboard Works*, New York, Dover Publications, 1988; *Quatrième livre de pièces de Clavecin* by François Couperin, Courlay, France, editions J. M. Fuzeau, 1987.
27. Couperin, *L'Art de toucher...*, page 24.
28. Thurston Dart, *The Interpretation of the Seventeenth and Eighteenth Century Music*, page 293.
29. *Ibid.*, page 23. See Girolamo Frescobaldi, *Organ and Keyboard Works, Volume III, The First Book of Toccatas and Partitas*, etc. 1637, complete edition by Pierre Pidoux, Kassel, Preface, page 1, 7th paragraph, Germany 1961. See also Arnold Dolmetsch, *The Interpretation of the Music of the Seventeenth and Eighteenth Centuries*, London, 1941, page 21.
30. Couperin, *L'Art de toucher...*, page 24.
31. *Ibid.*
32. *Ibid.*, page 33.
33. *Ibid.*, page 23.

3. German Treatises of the Eighteenth Century

1. C. P. E. Bach, *Versuch...*, paragraph 11.
2. *Ibid.*, paragraph 15, page 20.
3. *Ibid.*, Chapter 2, paragraph 9.
4. *Ibid.*, paragraph 11.
5. *Ibid.*, Chapter 3, paragraph 1.
6. *Ibid.*, paragraph 13.

4. Johann Sebastian Bach and Wolfgang Amadeus Mozart

1. Wolfgang Amadeus Mozart, *Briefe*, Berlin, 1964.
2. *Ibid.*, page 118.
3. *Ibid.*, page 298.

5. Frédéric Chopin and Franz Liszt

1. Carl Friedrich Weitzman, *Geschichte des Klavierspiels und Klavierliteratur*, Stuttgart, 1863, page 140.
2. James Gibbons Huneker, *Chopin. Czlowiek i artysta* (Chopin, The Man and the Artist), Lwów-Poznań (Lvov), 1922, page 70.
3. *Ibid.*
4. *Ibid.*
5. Mateusz Gliński, *Szopen* (Chopin), Monograph, Warsaw, 1932, page 76.
6. Jan Kleczyński, *Frederyck Chopin: Trois conférences fait à Warsovie*, Paris, 1880, page 34.
7. Gliński, *op. cit.*, page 75.
8. *Ibid.*
9. *Ibid.*, page 77; the same is in Kleczyński, *op. cit.*, page 47.
10. Kleczyński, *op. cit.*, page 34.
11. Huneker, *op. cit.*, page 74.
12. *Ibid.*, page 75.
13. *Ibid.*, page 78.
14. *Ibid.*, page 39.
15. Karol Mikuli, Preface to *Chopins Werke*, edition by the German firm of F. Kistner, page 3.
16. Kleczyński, *op. cit.*, page 40.
17. *Ibid.*
18. *Ibid.*
19. *Ibid.*, page 38, last score.
20. Kleczyński, "Notizzen zur Méthode des Méthodes," in *Chopins Grössere Werke*, Leipzig, 1898, pages 3-5.
21. Huneker, *op. cit.*, page 72. The same in Kleczyński, *Notizzen...*, pages 3-5.
22. *Ibid.*, page 72.
23. Kleczyński, *Frederyck Chopin...*, page 45.
24. Gliński, *op. cit.*, page 76.
25. Kleczyński, *Frederyck Chopin...*, page 52.
26. *Ibid.*, page 47.
27. Huneker, *Chopin...*, page 71.
28. *Ibid.*, page 72.
29. Wanda Chmielowska, *Z zagadnień nauczania gry na fortepiane* (From Questions of Learning to Play the Piano), Kraków, 1963, page 50.
30. Kleczyński, *Frederyck Chopin...*, page 81.
31. Chmielowska, *op. cit.*, page 51.
32. Huneker, *op. cit.*, page 54.
33. Gliński, *op. cit.*, page 74.
34. Huneker, *Chopin...*, page 269.
35. Gliński, *op. cit.*, page 75.
36. Huneker, *op. cit.*, page 267.
37. Kleczyński, *Frederyck Chopin...*, page 75.
38. Huneker, *op. cit.*, page 266.
39. *Ibid.*
40. Kleczyński, *Frederyck Chopin...*, page 80.
41. *Ibid.*, page 65.
42. *Ibid.*, page 66.
43. *Ibid.*, page 69.

44. *Ibid.*
45. *Ibid.*
46. *Ibid.*, page 72.
47. Carl Adolph Martienssen, *Schöpferischer Klavierunterricht,* Leipzig, 1954, page 45.
48. Kleczyński, *Frederyck Chopin*..., page 54.
49. *Ibid.*, page 57.
50. *Ibid.*, page 59.
51. Stanislaw Tarnowski, "Chopin—Posthumously," *Przegląd Polski* (Polish Review), Kraków, April, May, June, 1895.
52. Auguste Caroline Butini Boissier, *Franz Liszt als Lehrer,* Berlin, 1930, page 97.
53. *Ibid.*, page 66.
54. *Ibid.*
55. *Ibid.*
56. *Ibid.*, page 11.
57. *Ibid.*, pages 56 and 66.
58. *Ibid.*, page 56.
59. *Ibid.*
60. *Ibid.*, page 83.
61. *Ibid.*, page 96.
62. *Ibid.*
63. *Ibid.*, page 20.
64. *Ibid.*, page 112.
65. *Ibid.*, page 109.
66. *Ibid.*, 23rd lesson, March 13th.
67. *Ibid.*, page 28.
68. *Ibid.*
69. Weitzmann, *op. cit.*, page 164.
70. Boissier, *op. cit.*, page 112.
71. *Ibid.*, page 43.
72. *Ibid.*, page 57.
73. *Ibid.*, pages 107-108.
74. *Ibid.*, page 29.
75. *Ibid.*, pages 66 and 105.
76. *Ibid.*, page 34.
77. *Ibid.*, page 47.
78. *Ibid.*, page 29.
79. Julius Kapp, *Liszt,* Berlin, 1924, page 111.
80. Boissier, *op. cit.*, pages 21, 22, 23, and 24.
81. Kapp, *op. cit.*, page 112.
82. *Ibid.*
83. *Ibid.*, page 36.
84. Weitzmann, *op. cit.*, page 164.
85. Kapp, *op. cit.*, page 112.
86. *Ibid.*
87. *Ibid.*, page 113.
88. *Ibid.*, pages 111-112.
89. Weitzmann, *op. cit.*, page 163.
90. Karol Klindworth, *Elementar-Klavierschule,* Mainz, preface.
91. *Ibid.*
92. Kapp, *op. cit.*, page 111.

6. German and French Treatises of the Nineteenth Century

1. Wanda Chmielowska, *Z zagadnień nauczania gry na fortepiane* (From Questions of Learning to Play the Piano), Kraków, 1963, page 68.
2. Augusta Boissier, *Franz Liszt als Lehrer*, Berlin, 1930, Introduction.
3. N. Milstein, *Liszt*, Part II, Moscow, 1956, page 72.

Bibliography

Bach, Carl Phillip Emmanuel. *Versuch über die wahre Art das Klavier zu spielen.* Berlin: 1753. Facsimile, Leipzig: 1957.
Bie, Oscar. *Das Klavier.* Monaco: 1898.
Böhmová, Z. *Kapitoly z dějin klavírních škol.* Prague: 1973.
Boissier, Auguste Caroline Butini. *Franz Liszt als Lehrer.* Berlin: 1930.
Breithaupt, Rudolph Marie. *Die naturliche Klaviertechnik.* Leipzig: 1905.
Chmielowska, Wanda. *Z zagadnień nauczania gry na fortepiane.* Kraków: 1963.
Clementi, Muzio. *Gradus ad Parnassum.* Opus 44. The Second London Pianoforte School: after 1970.
Couperin, François. *L'Art de toucher le clavecin.* Leipzig: 1933. (3-lingual translation.)
Dolmetsch, A. *Interpretace hudby 17 a 18 storočia.* Prague: 1958.
Eigeldinger, Jean-Jacques, ed. *Chopin: Pianist and Teacher as Seen by His Pupils.* Third English Edition. New York: Cambridge University Press, 1988.
Forkel, J. N. *Über das Leben, die Kunst und Kunstwerke von Johann Sebastian Bach.* Leipzig: 1802.
Frescobaldi, Girolamo. *The First Book of Toccatas.* Facsimile. 2203 Bärenreuter Verlag, Kassel: 1961.
Gliński, Mateusz. *Szopen.* Monograph. Warsaw: 1932.
Huneker, James Gibbons. *Chopin. Czlowiek i artysta.* Lwów-Poznań (Lvov): 1922.
Kapp, Julius. *Liszt.* Berlin: 1911, 1922, 1924.
Kleczyński, Jan. *Frederyck Chopin: Trois conférences fait à Warsovie.* Paris: 1880.
_____. "Notizzen zur Méthode des Méthodes," in *Chopins Grössere Werke.* Leipzig: 1898.
_____. "Szopen jako nauczyciel fortepianu," *Bluszcz,* No. 5, 1869.
Klindworth, Karol. *Elementar-Klavierschule.* Mainz.
Kullak, Adolph. *Aesthetik des Klavierspiels.* Berlin: 1860; Leipzig: 1922.
Lussy, Mathis. *Traité de l'expression musicale.* Paris: 1874.
Maeckel, O. V. *Das organische Klavierspiel.* Iserlohm: 1938.
Martienssen, Carl Adolph. *Schöpferischer Klavierunterricht.* Leipzig: 1954.
Michalowski, Aleksander. "Jak gral Chopin in Mateusz Gliński," in *Szopen.* Warsaw: 1932.
Mikuli, Karol. Preface to *Chopins Werke.* Edition by the German firm F. Kistner: n.d.
Milstein. *Liszt.* Moscow: 1956.
Modr, A. *Hudební nástroje.* Prague: 1977.
Mozart, Wolfgang Amadeus. *Briefe.* Berlin: 1964.
Nikolajev, Aleksander. *Oczerki po mietodike obuczenia igry na fortepiano.* Moscow: 1977, 1983.
Pociej, Bohdan. *Klavesyniści francuscy, Polskie wydawnictwo muzyczne.* Kraków: 1969.

Shchapov, Arsenij. *Fortepiannyj urok v muzykalnoj shkole i uchilishche.* Moscow: 1947.
Steinhausen, Friedrich Adolph. *Die physiologischen Fehler und die Umgestaltung der Klaviertechnik.* Leipzig: 1905.
Tarnowski, Stanislav. "Chopin—Posthumously," *Przegląd polski.* Kraków: April, May, June, 1895.
Türk, Daniel Gottlob. *Klavierschule oder Anweisung zum Klavierspielen für Lehrer und Lehrnende.* Leipzig: 1798.
Varrö, Margit. *Der lebendige Klavierunterricht.* Leipzig: 1929.
Weitzmann, Carl Friederich. *Geschichte des Klavierspiels und Klavierliteratur.* Stuttgart: 1863.

Index

Accelerendo 162-165, 168, 170
Accentuation, accented notes (tones) 68, 75, 77-79, 81, 103, 118, 148-150, 154-158, 161, 170
Acciaccatura 72, 73
Aeolus 138
Aesthetic interpretation 148
Agogic accent 79
Agogics, agogic device 19, 24, 60, 85, 86, 92, 117, 122, 152, 170
Albert, E. 126
Allemande 28
Alteration 159-161
Ammerbach, E. 16
Applicature *see* Fingering
Appoggiatura (Port de voix) 8, 19, 21-23, 27, 35, 49, 55, 71-73, 76
Appoggiatura, long (Accented vorschlag) 19, 53, 55, 57, 58, 77
Appoggiatura, short 23, 53, 57, 66, 72
Appoggiatura, unaccented (Nachschlag) 51, 53, 72, 78
Arsis 157
Articulation x, 91, 93, 106, 107, 114, 131
Articulatory device 31

Bach, C. 11, 12, 17, 21, 23, 37-41, 42-67, 70, 71, 73, 74, 77, 87, 89, 91, 95, 96, 99
Bach, J. 11, 12, 17-19, 23, 31, 38, 42, 46, 47, 49, 53, 55, 57, 61, 65, 87, 89, 90-96, 112, 114, 116, 117, 128, 137, 142, 145, 148
Bach, W. 53, 87
Bar (measure) 150, 151

Bartok, B. 68
Batteries (Arpeggios) 13, 15
Beat 150
Bebung (Vibrato) 1, 41, 66, 72, 73, 93
Bechstein (piano) 137
Beethoven, L. 38, 104, 114, 116, 142, 148, 149, 157, 161, 163-169
Bellini, V. 167
Berlioz, H. 118, 151
Bermudo, J. 33, 47
Bischoff, H. 141
Boissier, A. 126-135, 146, 151
Brahms, J. 151
Breithaupt, R. 12, 113, 143, 145
Bronsart, H. 133, 139
Büchner, H. 16
Büllow, H. 126, 151

Caland 143
Cantabile (style) 63, 94, 139
Chambonnières, J. 5, 8, 19
Chopin, F. 11, 35, 47, 48, 58, 86, 101-131, 143, 145, 146, 150, 151, 155, 160, 165, 169
Church modes 93
Clark, J. 143
Clavichord 1, 38, 39, 41, 52, 63, 65, 66, 88, 92, 93, 96, 98
Clementi, M. 38, 112, 114, 142
Combination ornament 57
Coulé (slide) 23, 30, 36, 49, 53, 72, 73
Counting 151
Couperin, F. 7, 11-19, 21-26, 29-36, 39, 41, 42, 45, 46, 49, 50, 51, 55, 60, 63, 65, 66, 71, 72, 79, 85, 86, 88, 93-96

181

INDEX

Couperin, L. 27, 28
Cramer, B. 114, 142
Creative will 144
Czartoryska, M. 101, 102, 104, 116-118, 125, 126
Czerny, C. 38, 108, 127, 142

Dandrieu J. 8
D'Anglebert, J. 8, 19, 27, 28
Dart, T. 28
Debussy, C. 35
Denise, J. 6
Deppe 143
Descant (soprano melody) 132
Diatonic system 93
Diruta, G. 35
Displaced and stolen time 85
Dissonances 49, 63, 76-78, 124, 159, 161
Draeseke, F. 137, 138
Drop and lift (Mannheim sigh) 63, 66, 76, 78
Dussek (Dusík), J. 114, 142

Ekier, J. 117
Embellishments (ornaments, ornamentation) 49, 50-53, 64, 71, 73, 74, 86, 119
English fingering 109
Enharmonic modulations 125
Études 94, 114, 132

Fermata 38
Field, J. 114, 164
Figured bass 38, 39, 75, 95
Figuring 15
Filtsch 101
Fingering 108, 109, 111, 112, 152
Fioritures (ornamentational small notes) 125
Fischer, E. 142
Földess, A. 34
Forkel, J. 87, 89, 90-94, 96
Forte pedal (right pedal) 123, 125

Fortepiano (Hammerclavier) 1, 38, 39, 41, 52, 59, 65, 86, 88, 93, 98
Franchôme 104
Free fantasia 38, 39
French fingering 109
French pianos 104
Frescobaldi, G. 18

Gaultier, D. 27
German method 105
Gestaltungsville (driving force) 122
Gevaert, F. 153
Gieseking, W. 113
Gliński, M. 102, 123
Gottschalk, L. 101
Gounod, C. 160, 167
Grupetti (ornamental notes) 119
Gutman, A. 101

Hammerschlag 146
Händel, G. 18, 114
Harmonization 39, 105
Harmony 95
Harpsichord (Cembalo, Clavicembalo, Clavecin) 2, 38, 39, 41, 63, 65, 66, 92, 93, 137
Hartmann, K. 101
Haydn, J. 38, 65, 67, 126, 142
Hegel, F. 136
Henselt, T. 150
Hervelois, C. 50
Hiller, S. 114
Holistic idea 152
Honneger, A. 150
Hummel, J. 97, 114, 142
Huneker, J. 102, 104, 105, 151

Intelligence (musical intelect) 125, 133, 155, 156
Interpretation x, 91

Jaël 143

INDEX 183

Kalkbrenner, F. 109, 127
Kapp, J. 136
Kleczyński, J. 102, 104–107, 112, 120, 123, 125
Klindworth, K. 126, 139, 140
Kullak, A. 108, 113, 141–145, 150–153

Lambert, M. 6, 8
Law of contrast 167, 168
Legato playing 123, 146
Leimer, H. 113
Leszetycki, J. 113
Light quilling 10
Liszt, F. 11, 35, 101, 104, 118, 123, 126–140, 143, 144, 146, 147, 151, 155
Lussy, M. 12, 122, 153–170
Lute structure 5
Lützow 98
Lysberg, K. 101

Maeckl, O. 138
Mälzel, J. 69
Marais, M. 50
Marpurg, F. 19, 37, 145
Martienssen, C. 122, 138, 144
Mathias, G. 101, 102
Matthay 143
Meara, C. 101, 102
Mechanics 143, 144
Melodic unit (musical thought) 80–84
Memorization (musical memory) 134, 143, 144, 152
Mendelssohn, F. 104, 114
Metric 150, 151
Metric accentuation 155–157, 159, 161, 168
Meyerbeer, G. 118, 159
Michalowski, A. 102, 104, 107, 117, 118
Milstein, N. 151
Minidynamics 63
Modulation (modulation tones) 77, 163, 169
Mondonville, J. 19
Mordent 20, 23, 27, 49, 53, 56, 72, 73
Moscheles, I. 114, 127, 132, 142
Motorik 4, 12, 17, 65

Mozart, W. 11, 65, 67, 85, 87, 97–99, 104, 114, 117, 118, 126, 142, 150, 162–164, 166–168
Music dynamics 168, 170
Musical expression 153–155, 169, 170
Musical idea (phrase, thought) 152, 156, 157, 161, 163, 164, 168–170
Musical (aural) imagination 170
Musical punctuation 74, 75, 77, 79–82; punctuation marks (caesuras) 81–83, 86
Musical sentence 94, 119, 120, 122
Musical space (stratum) 134

Neugauz, S. 3
Niemann, W. 141
Nikolajev, A. 108
Nivers, G. 8
Non-measured preludes 27

Old schools 142, 143, 150
Organ 88

Paganini, N. 135
Pasquini, D. 150
Pathetic (emotional) accents 155, 158–162, 168
Paumann, C. 16
Pearly play 146
Pearly effect 89, 105
Pedal, pedaling 105, 115, 122–125, 147, 152, 162, 170
Peruzzi, E. 101
Phrasing (phrase see also Musical punctuation) x, 91, 92, 102, 103, 115, 117–121, 134, 148, 152, 155, 162, 168
Phrasing devices 36
Piano pedal (left pedal) 125
Potocka, D. 101
Pralltriller (upper mordent) 22, 23, 35, 49, 53, 54, 56, 65, 72, 73
Progressions 13
Prokofiev, S. 150

Purcell, H. 19
Purposeful technique 143

Quantz, J. 69

Rallentando 165-168
Rameau, J. 3, 7, 8, 12, 13, 19, 25, 42, 50, 108
Rappoldi, L. 136-138, 140
Rejcha, A. 132, 155
Relaxation of hands 103, 113, 139, 144
Rhythmic accents 155-157, 159, 168
Richards, B. 101
Riemann, H. 84
Ries, H. 114
Rosenthal, A. 126
Rossini, G. 160, 167, 168
Rubinstein 137, 142
Rubio, V. 101
Rule of modulation 169

Santa Maria, T. 33
Scarlatti, D. 114, 137, 142
Schönberg, A. 142
Schumann, G. 101
Schumann, R. 114, 136, 140
Scriabin, A. 149, 151
Shschapov, A. 133
Singing legato 122
Singing melody (cantilena) 124, 147, 149
Sloper, L. 101
Slurred thirds 14, 36
Sonority 168, 169
Springer 23
Stein, R. 97-99
Steinbrecher, W. 101
Steinhausen, F. 12, 113, 143, 144
Steininger 143
Streicher, F. 101, 102
Sulzer, J. 83
Suspension and aspiration 19, 24, 25, 33, 35, 36, 79, 85, 86

Sygietyński, A. 116
Syncopated notes 77
Syncopated pedal 124, 162-164, 166

Tablatura 9, 10, 47
Tarnowski, S. 102, 125
Tausig, C. 126, 135
Tellefsen, T. 101
Tempered piano 93
Tempo rubato 35, 84, 85, 98, 102, 104-119, 150, 151, 161
Tetzel 143
Thalberg, S. 123
Theory of affect 64, 153
Theory of time 69
Theses 163
Thorough bass 38, 39
Timbre (tone color) 114, 137, 139, 147, 148, 152
Time (measure bar tempo) 67, 69, 92, 105, 118, 134, 150, 155, 156, 158, 159, 161-164, 167, 170
Touch (attack) xi, 11, 12, 65, 91, 94, 95, 101, 103-105, 107, 111, 112, 114, 116, 127, 128, 137, 139, 146, 147
Türk, D. 11, 37, 38, 63, 65, 66-86, 99, 145
Turn 57, 72, 73

Varrö, M. 144
Verdi, G. 160
Vogler 98, 99

Weber, C. 114, 150
Weitzmann, G. 131, 138-140
Wernik, K. 101
Wiedeburg, F. 37
Wolf, G. 37

Zaleska, Z. 101, 102